The Complete Guide to a Successful Cruise

Jeraldine Saunders

iUniverse.com, Inc.
San Jose New York Lincoln Shanghai

The Complete Guide to a Successful Cruise

All Rights Reserved © 1978, 2000 by Jeraldine Saunders

No part of this book may be reproduced or transmitted in any form or by any means, graphic, electronic, or mechanical, including photocopying, recording, taping, or by any information storage retrieval system, without the permission in writing from the publisher.

Published by iUniverse.com, Inc.

For information address:
iUniverse.com, Inc.
5220 S 16th, Ste. 200
Lincoln, NE 68512
www.iuniverse.com

Originally published by Contemporary Books

The information and material contained in this book are provided "as is," without warranty of any kind, express or implied, including without limitation any warranty concerning the accuracy, adequacy, or completeness of such information or material or the results to be obtained from using such information or material. Neither iUniverse.com, Inc., nor the author shall be responsible for any claims attributable to errors, omissions, or other inaccuracies in the information or material contained in this book, and in no event shall iUniverse.com, Inc. or the author be liable for direct, indirect, special, incidental, or consequential damages arising out of the use of such information or material.

ISBN: 0-595-14779-8

Printed in the United States of America

Dedicated to Gael
and all my former and future passengers
who sail with me.

A special thank you to Arthur Andrews
and to my assistant Miss Lynette Vogt
and my literary agents Doris and Reece Halsey

Contents

    Foreword   vii
    Preface   xiii
    Ten Commandments for Passengers   xv
1. Bon Voyage: Anticipation, Preparation, and Boarding   1
2. When the Sun Comes Up   11
3. The Dining Room   15
4. Cruise Clothes: Getting All Decked Out   27
5. Let Us Entertain You   33
6. Ports of Call   55
7. Traveling Unattached   59
8. Cruise Etiquette   61
9. Vim and Vigor: Health Tips for Cruise Passengers   63
10. The Art of Traveling   69
11. The Joy of Shopping on the Bounding Main   71
12. What to Do If You Find Yourself on the *Leaking Lena*   75

CONTENTS

13 Guidelines on Tipping   77
14 The Distinctive Language of the Sea   79
15 Displacement and Tonnage   93
16 Classification Societies   97
17 Turnaround   99
18 Disembarkation   101
19 Immigration   103
20 Cruising Pictorialized: The Dream Merchants   105
21 Customs Hints for Returning U.S. Residents   135
22 Until We Meet Again   167
    Index   169

Foreword

The first time I met Jeraldine Saunders I met her twice.

I was struggling to get into my life jacket during boat drill the first morning out. As usual, I was all thumbs. Jeraldine Saunders, all woman, came to my rescue.

"Why, I know you!" said the vibrant Virgo, tossing her auburn hair and flashing her big green eyes. "Weren't you on the *Princess Carla* three years ago on a Caribbean cruise?"

Face to face with the flattery of recognition from this uncommonly beautiful lady with the uncommonly long memory, this Aquarian momentarily lost his sea legs, forgot that his favorite color is ocean-blue, and mumbled a reply. Yes, he stammered, he did recall the ship and the trip. But he didn't remember *her* because

FOREWORD

he'd spent all of his time in his cabin hunched over a humid Underwood, working.

"Working?" she smiled. "Don't you know cruise ships are for having fun?"

Since then, of course, I've learned the wisdom of her words. And in almost a quarter-century of jet-age travel and travel writing, I've come to know what Miss Saunders and millions of other passengers down the shipping lanes of time always have known: Travel by cruise ship is the most relaxing, romantic, and regal way to go—whether round the corner on a three-day party cruise or round the world on a three-month odyssey.

"And to our age's drowsy blood still shouts the inspiring sea. . . ."

What exactly causes man and woman to go down to the sea in ships, to succumb to sea fever, to surrender to the lissome Loreleis who, like Jeraldine Saunders, lure us from our snug harbors onto the sometimes rocky but always irresistibly restful cradle of the deep?

Byron can tell you. Or Conrad. Or Melville. Or Nordhoff and Hall. Or Barry Cornwall, who proclaims: "The sea! the sea! the open sea! The blue, the fresh, the ever free!"

Freedom. . . .

There's a lot of talk these computerized days about losing our identity, our freedom. But there's one place on earth you don't have to worry about losing yours: on the sea. The freedom from care, the freedom to come and go as you please, the freedom to do as much or as little as you choose—nowhere in the world is such freedom rampant as on a passenger ship sailing the open sea.

Once your liner pulls away from the pier, you are cut free from care as neatly as the bon-voyage party serpentine is severed from the receding vessel itself. The pressures of life disappear over the horizon. You are

Foreword

free from deadlines and headlines, telephones and traffic, diapers and dirty dishes. The fresh sea breeze frees your lungs from smog and the deck sports free your aging sinews from the kinks of office desk or housemaid's knee.

You're free to be a lover. Or a loner. Shall I mix with the throng or curl up with the book I've always meant to read? The choice is yours and the freedom is there to do either or neither or both. You are free to sit on the bridge deck and watch the skipper plough a path through exotic waters, or to sit at the bridge table until you see nothing but spots before your eyes.

You are free to stand at the rail and watch the seabirds soar and the flying fishes play, and perhaps wonder what gems of purest ray serene, the dark unfathomed caves of ocean bear. You can give free rein to your imagination as the waves bound rhythmically beneath you like a horse who knows his rider. Passengers too shy or rusty to dance on shore kick up a storm at sea after a lesson or two with the hostess. Talent night? Why not give it a whirl—you've nothing to lose but your inhibitions. Besides, your voice always did deserve more than a shower stall. Costume party? Do your own thing and let the crepe paper fall where it may.

You also can give free rein to your appetite, and no one's there to nag you if you fall off the diet wagon again. With early morning coffee, followed by breakfast, followed by mid-morning bouillon, followed by luncheon, followed by afternoon tea, followed by dinner, followed by midnight buffet . . . well, one would have to be deaf indeed not to hear freedom ring when the dinner bell does.

Want to sleep 'til noon? Host a cocktail party at midnight? Go ahead. Want to feel and look important? Dress up for dinner. Hobnob with the captain and officers. Rub elbows with all those other important

FOREWORD

people—ships are loaded to the gunwales with celebrities these days. What's more, you really can make friends with fellow passengers and crew. Aboard an airliner at 600 miles an hour, friendships are fleeting; on an ocean liner, they can be forever.

"I'm still friendly with passengers I had 15 years ago," a room steward once told me. "I'm on a lot of mailing lists." And, confided a little old lady taking afternoon tea on the promenade deck on, believe it or not, her 22nd voyage: "I have more friends at sea than I do ashore. A cruise is better than a class reunion."

In short, people who need people are the luckiest people in the world, and twice as lucky if they're on an ocean voyage. Cruise ships truly are "friend" ships.

Best of all, on a Love Boat you're free to fall in love—for keeps or until the next port. With the handsome purser or the mysterious gal in saucer sunglasses and saucy bikini. (And don't forget the ocean always looks better when you're holding hands, especially at night when the stars reach down to human height.)

Or you can fall in love with the sea itself, which can be the biggest romance of all.

Cruise-ship travel also frees you from the tedium of hotel-hopping, the ceaseless packing and unpacking, the scurrying around for souvenirs (they're all there in one neat little duty-free shipboard shop, or in handy stores ashore). And you are free of frenzied crowds and the endless climbing on and off sightseeing buses and the worries of making connections and the mind-fogging confusion of jet lag.

And now that you've read this far in the introduction, you're finally free to plunge into the tempting waters of Jeraldine Saunders' newest book. All the questions I've been asked as a travel editor—and many that went unasked—she answers with the expertise that comes from working 19 hours a day, seven days a

Foreword

week, 11 months a year for 8 years as one of the world's foremost cruise directors.

I know no one better qualified to write this book. Maybe it's her diet of health food and Vitamin E that does it. Maybe it's because she doesn't drink ("I get high on people," she told me). Maybe it's the astrology (she'll read your palm at the drop of a falling star).

But just as she retains the same slender figure and dress size she boasted for 20 years as a high-fashion model, so this ageless temptress retains the enthusiasm, energy, ebullience, knowledge, and charm that should stir *your* drowsy blood to answer the ageless call of the sea.

Morton Cathro
Moraga, California
February 1978

(Morton Cathro, now entertainment editor of the *Oakland Tribune*, was its travel editor and columnist for 23 years. He has held top posts with the Society of American Travel Writers, and has contributed to many newspapers, magazines, and travel anthologies. Among his several national awards are first place in the 29th annual Trans World Airlines writing competition, and the $1,000 grand prize given by the Pacific Cruise Conference for the year's best stories on ship travel. An interview with Jeraldine Saunders was one of his winning entries.)

Preface

First time passengers on the maze of decks, amid the crowded sophistication of a luxury cruise ship, hate to be constantly asking about the things the seasoned passengers already know.

Embarrassment is an uncomfortable feeling, so anything that will relieve it, social, financial, or imaginary, is a welcome gift to the inexperienced voyager.

You will find information here that no other book has ever given—advice that your best friends will not—or rather—just *cannot* tell you.

I am sharing hints and secrets which I have gathered from living aboard cruise ships seven days a week, eleven months a year for over eight years.

I suggest you read this book before sailing and keep it in your cabin for reference during sailing. Study it carefully, then sail along the decks with confidence and

PREFACE

joy, for now your ship will surely become a "Love Boat."

Jeraldine Saunders
Glendale, California

Ten Commandments for Passengers

1. Do not expect to find things as they were at home, for you have left home in order to find them different!

2. Take nothing too seriously, for a carefree mind is the essence of a vacation!

3. Do not let the other passengers get on your nerves, for you have paid good money to have a good time!

4. Remember you have control over your attitude and it will determine your happiness on shipboard, or in port!

5. Remember to say THANK YOU, for those words are more cherished than a tip.

6. Learn to make change in the currency of each port that you shall not be cheated!

7. Do not worry, for worry is the enemy of pleasure.

TEN COMMANDMENTS FOR PASSENGERS

8. When in Rome, do as Romans do—tempered always by your native common sense and friendliness!

9. Do not base your judgment of the people of a country by the actions of one troublesome individual.

10. Remember, thou art a guest in all other lands. And whoever treats the host with respect shall in turn be an honored guest!

1

Bon Voyage: Anticipation, Preparation, and Boarding

We are always getting ready to live, but never living.
—Ralph Waldo Emerson

Travel is one thing, but cruising is another! It is a holiday like no other. Your "Welcome Aboard!" really begins long before you actually step onto the gangway.

I feel it starts when your travel agent hands you your ticket. The "Foretaste" begins to build. Ahead lies the prospect of a brief but thrilling life on the briny sea, away from the treadmill of work or routine, the noise of the freeways, and pressures of your day-to-day life.

You, possessing the spirit of adventure, are now going to be one of the chosen inhabitants of a world utterly different and apart. Fantasy land is about to be yours!

But come down to earth long enough to study in earnest the suggestions that follow and yours will be a cruise to be remembered indeed!

Start by devoting some time to thoroughly going over all the information that comes with your ticket.

Did you receive enough baggage tags? If you didn't, call the cruise line or your travel agent and ask to have more mailed to you.

I want to impress upon you the importance of tagging *every* piece of baggage you plan to take with you. Be sure your first and last name are printed on the tags along with your cabin number. I could write TV scripts from now till doomsday about the crazy things that happen to passengers when they have to spend the first night at sea with just their "bon voyage" gag gifts because their luggage was placed on board without tags and cabin numbers on them. Most ships have foreign crews who may have trouble reading your name, so writing down your cabin number is a must—a *double* must!

Now is the time to make sure that your name is spelled correctly on your ticket because this is the way it will appear on the souvenir passenger list which is usually distributed a few days after sailing.

In your ticket packet, you will find a card with mail and radiogram information. It will show how letters to you should be addressed in care of the various port agents. Ships have agents in every port. Their names and addresses will be listed on this card.

The card will also explain how you can be contacted by radiogram (cable). Radiograms are accepted only while your ship is sailing. Ships are not allowed to have ship-to-shore telephone service while in port; this is an international law. You will have to go ashore to telephone while your ship is in port.

Next, check the sailing date on your ticket and—this is very important—be sure the correct cabin number has been written on the ticket.

It is also a good idea to study the deck plan thoroughly and learn the location of your cabin in relation to the other areas of the ship. Knowing the location and number of your cabin is important for your friends and

A sea gulls' view of Sitmar Cruise's *Fairwind*.

relatives, too, when they come to see you off. Because passengers usually board separately from their visitors, you will want to be able to tell them beforehand, where to meet you.

Your ticket envelope will contain boarding passes for visitors. Again if you need more, ask your friendly travel agent.

It's fun to invite friends to your cabin for a bon voyage party. A cruise send-off in the "grand manner" will include all the friends that you might wish and

Spacious cabins are standard aboard the S.S. *Doric* (Home Lines, Inc.).

plenty of champagne, and canapes. Your stateroom (cabin) will serve as the center of activities, but if you overflow into one of the lounges, that's fine too. A bon voyage party request form is usually included in the ticket packet. Just fill yours out and send it to the ship line (*at least* 3 or 4 days prior to sailing). The ship's caterers will do all the rest. Although you can order all the trimmings for this party from the shipping line, many passengers have friends who bring their own hors d'oeuvres and champagne to the party with them. Some guests arrive with ingeniously wrapped gifts and bottles of champagne. Meanwhile porters will be scurrying about trying to deliver baggage to the proper cabins. Stewards will be balancing trays of canapes and buckets of ice through alleyways filled with happy people. Live music from the ballroom and nightclubs will add to the tempo, trebling the excitement to a joyous frenzy.

Bon Voyage

On some ships, if you are having an exceptionally large party, you may request one of the private lounges for your bon voyage.

A word of caution: Make sure your visitors are off the ship 30 minutes prior to sailing time. Announcements will be made over the public address system that "All visitors must go ashore—the ship is about to sail." But sometimes a visitor, caught up in all the gaiety and high spirits of the occasion, forgets to get off the ship in time. (It's a costly trip by pilot boat from ship to shore.)

You may also arrange for other special occasions, such as birthdays and anniversaries, through the reservations office of the cruise line or through your travel agent prior to departure. Or, you may make these arrangements en route by notifying the purser's office or the maitre d'.

Friends who are unable to attend your shipboard bon voyage party will be interested to learn about a service called Well Wishers, International. They provide on-board delivery. Orders placed up to twelve hours prior to sailing are "unconditionally guaranteed." The standard selections are: Candy, fancy dried fruits, fruit baskets, gourmet pastries, floral arrangements, and, of course, champagne. The owner, Mort Walco, also sends special gift pack requests for children, diabetics, and people with unique tastes. Example: he arranged for and delivered to a honeymooning couple a Volkswagen filled with flowers!

Details and free brochures are available from Well Wishers, International, 107 West College Street, Covina, California 91723.

Check your ticket for boarding time. Allow yourself ample time to get to the pier, but please don't get there several hours in advance of the official check-in time. Passengers are *not* allowed to board until the official embarkation time set by the cruise line, and this is a firm rule. Earlier cruise passengers will have just disembarked, and the crew must completely clean and prepare the entire ship for your cruise. In addition, ship stores have to be loaded. So with all this preparation going on, you can understand why you can't go aboard earlier than stated on your ticket. In some terminals, there will be a waiting lounge area with some chairs.

Before you leave home or your hotel, be sure to have your cruise ticket, passport (if needed), and any other necessary documents all together and easily accessible—in your handbag or pocket. This will smooth your way through the "check-in" by the cruise company representatives who process your embarkation on the pier.

While you are proceeding with this check-in, expect lots of smiling faces in line with you. Each is looking at the other anticipating and knowing that they are all here for one reason only—enjoyment! A camaraderie begins here.

Meanwhile porters are taking your luggage aboard for delivery to your cabin. These porters are employed by the cruise line to handle baggage. It is customary but not obligatory to tip them. The amount should depend upon how much baggage you have. These porters are not part of the crew, they are dock workers.

After the check-in on the pier, you are at last ready to go aboard!

As you step off the gangway, you will receive a friendly greeting from one of the members of the cruise staff, either the cruise director or one of his assistants. These include cruise hostess, the assistant cruise director, one of the members of the dance team, or the sports director.

Next comes the ship's photographer. He'll ask you to "look this way," so be prepared with a big smile. A day or two later, your photograph will appear with those of

Bon Voyage

your fellow passengers on the photographer's bulletin board, which is always located in one of the most frequented parts of the ship.

The ship's photographers are a breed unto themselves. On a three-day cruise when photos must be developed and displayed on time or all is lost, they work round-the-clock. Their photos, which are taken throughout the cruise, may be viewed on the display board. All are numbered for easy ordering.

Now you move on into the lobby or foyer of the ship where immaculately groomed stewards are waiting to escort you to your cabin.

Businesslike but charming accommodations on board Royal Caribbean Cruise Line ships.

THE COMPLETE GUIDE TO A SUCCESSFUL CRUISE

Bon voyage festivities aboard a Prudential cruise.

Once you've inspected your cabin, don't unpack; go without delay to the dining salon and arrange your table reservations with the maitre d'. Tell him your preference: a small table for two, or a large one where you will make new friends. (Refer to chapter 3 for more details.)

Now some of the most exciting days of your life are about to begin! To some, a cruise gives a cleansing feeling of being reborn and to others it gives a delightful feeling of enhanced sensual excitement. On shipboard, the power of the moon, which is associated with the ocean, seems to have a stronger effect on the body's fluids and emotions. When you are in the grip of nature's strongest force, you will find that all your appetites are stimulated. At the same time you will find that you are enjoying a deeper and more restful sleep, thanks to the lulling rise and fall of the sea.

Bon Voyage

The happy ending of a happy beginning—"bon voyage" on a Sitmar cruise.

THE COMPLETE GUIDE TO A SUCCESSFUL CRUISE

When you hear the announcement, "All visitors ashore, the ship is about to sail," scurry out on deck. It is truly exciting and fun to join your fellow passengers as they throw serpentine (it's a good idea to bring some of your own, for you may want more than is handed out) from the ship to their visitors now on shore. Meanwhile the sending-off parties are merrily tossing their streamers back until the ship appears to be caught in a giant multicolored web.

Usually, there is an orchestra on deck playing "Anchors Aweigh." Bright bits of confetti enliven the air. Visitors by the dock's rail shout and wave their goodbyes while the photographer snaps away! Never be afraid to ask the photographer to take a picture any time he is shooting because he will be more than eager to oblige.

The excitement reaches its peak when the long blast of the ship's whistle announces that the mooring lines have been released and are being brought aboard. Now you feel a gentle tug as the ship slips away from land—and your heart skips a beat as you feel the emotional intoxication that only the anticipation of a cruise can bring.

2

When the Sun Comes Up

There is no duty we underrate so much as the duty of being happy.
—Robert Louis Stevenson

God sends the sun each day and with God's help and the cruise director's sheer drive, the ship's program gets written each day.

I have been the world's only female cruise director, and I know what a hectic pace is necessary. I have worked on cruise ships seven days a week, eleven months a year for over eight years. I am a sailor. Although I was not a member of the crew or an officer of the ship, I was, as all cruise directors are, in charge of all the social activities and entertainment aboard ship. This includes managing the orchestras and planning daily programs. Another chore is making sure the printer (who usually doesn't speak English) gets the program printed and distributed, sometime between 11:00 P.M. and 4:00 A.M., so that upon awakening, you will find its friendly greeting under your cabin door.

Jeraldine entertains on board the M.S. *Donna Montserrat*, a Negros Navigation Company ship.

A crew show aboard a March Shipping Corporation vessel.

When the Sun Comes Up

This daily program contains loads of information and it's a good idea to fold it and keep it with you throughout the day. Then you won't miss any of the unique activities featured that day. (See chapter 5.) These activities are fun and offer you a wonderful opportunity to become acquainted with your fellow passengers and the cruise staff who are chosen for their ability to help you "let your hair down." Join in the fun, for the days that make us happy are the days that make us wise.

Recipe for Anticipation

You have thought much and made up your mind.
The vacation you've chosen is one of a kind.
Since it is seagoing, you wonder at its latitude.
That is very personal and depends solely on your
   attitude

SO

Think of the ocean and the sunsets galore,
Think of far places and exotic sights ashore,
Think of heavenly foods and constant pampering,
Think of peace—and freedom from tampering,
Think of peoples friendly—yet foreign to you,
Think of their lives and the things they do,
Think of the shops and the treasures you'll buy,
Think of the sunny beaches upon which you'll lie,
Think of seas bathed in blissful moonlight,
Think of romance—on such a stage—what delight,
Think of the ship dedicated wholly to your pleasure,
Think of the joy of experiencing absolute leisure.

REMEMBER

Think of these things—only you can make them come
   true.
Think them into reality—the cruise is meant especially
   for you!

—Arthur Andrews

3

The Dining Room

Life is a banquet but most sons of bitches are starving to death!
—Auntie Mame

The party is NEVER over; not in your ship's dining room!

The delicious hors d'oeuvres at your bon voyage party and every succeeding meal, including the last hurry-up breakfast just before your return to home port, will convince you that *your* cruise ship serves the most delicious food in the world!

Whether your ship is a magnificent floating palace or hardly larger than your average billionaire's yacht, your chef will be able to turn out a Cordon Bleu masterpiece or a simple grilled hamburger perfectly to your individual taste.

Seating arrangements

If you haven't already done so, hurry to the dining room (I've said this before, but it bears repeating) to reserve the table where you will take all meals during

The pleasures of the table on board a Sitmar cruise.

the voyage. You will meet with an important individual whose title—according to the national origin of the ship—may be director or manager of the dining room, maitre d' hôtel, or chief dining room steward.

It is proper when dining on shipboard to order as soon as your steward asks you. You needn't wait for the others assigned your table to arrive. They may have decided to eat in their cabin or wish to remain in the cocktail lounge a little longer. Do try to be on time for your meals. If you must arrive late, I suggest you skip the appetizers in order to catch up with the others.

If you have special diet requirements, or if you are planning onboard birthday or anniversary parties, now

The Dining Room

is the moment to discuss them with the maitre d', so he can make his preparations ... particularly if the cruise is a short-term one. You can also request decaffeinated coffee and diet desserts at this time.

Traveling alone? Want to meet people? If so, leave your seating to the discerning maitre d' for he is a skilled diplomat and social engineer. It will be his pleasure to place you with congenial table companions. We don't promise that he will find a Prince Charming for every unattached woman, but his matchmaking average is high! Usually a large table is best if you are traveling alone.

On the cruise, you may find a new friend, and want to move to his or her table. Tell the maitre d'; he'll do his best to comply. Remember to tip the waiter whose table you are leaving.

Sittings

If your ship's dining room is not large enough to accommodate all passengers at the same time, there may be first and second sittings.

Here is one ship's schedule, which is typical for those with two sittings.

Dining Room Schedule

First sitting		Second sitting	
Breakfast	7:45 A.M.	Breakfast	9 A.M.
Lunch	12 Noon	Lunch	1:30 P.M.
Dinner	6 P.M.	Dinner	8 P.M.

The first sitting, generally more informal, is ideal for families with young children, for people who want to eat and get the best seats at the early movie, and for those who are taking an ocean voyage in order to get a good rest. I always try to eat at the First Sitting because I get hungry early. After dinner, in the main salon, there are always two live entertainment shows, one for each sitting.

The second sitting is popular with passengers who want plenty of time to dress for the evening and to attend cocktail parties before dining.

Open sitting is a term that applies to times when you may sit wherever you please, such as during the first night's informal buffet or when the ship is in port.

Additional food options

Besides learning about the hours of your three regular meals, you will want to know about the availability of snacks and additional meals. Yes, you will! The stimuli of the bracing ocean air, the miles you'll walk on shore tours, and the hours you'll dance under the moon, will sharpen your appetite so that you'll pounce on every tray of goodies a steward carries past you!

Room service

Room service is ideal for honeymooners and other lovers or when you feel hungover or a little under par from climbing the pyramids, or if you arrive back on ship late from shore and miss a scheduled meal. Many passengers like to order breakfast from room service, so they can dress at their leisure. All meals and snacks on board are included in your fare, but it's nice to leave your steward an extra tip for this service.

A schedule of shipboard food service hours—those in addition to regular mealtimes—follows.

Early riser's coffee

About 6:30 A.M. the first cup of coffee is served in a public room or on deck. This service attracts people who have never gone to bed, lifelong early-risers, insomniacs, shore-excursioners, joggers, dawn-watchers, and navigation freaks. Don't miss it. Pastries and donuts are often included.

The Dining Room

Mid-morning snack (or elevenses)

Around 10–11 A.M. the deck stewards pass around a choice of bouillon, tomato juice, or fruit juices to those who cannot wait an hour or two until their scheduled lunch.

Special lunches

If the weather is fine, a buffet luncheon is often served on deck or poolside. The chef will present specialties as tempting to view as to chew! You'll find hollowed-out watermelons heaped with delicate portions of chilled tropical fruits, gelatin salads molded in the shape of giant fish, perhaps a swan carved out of ice bearing bite-sized bits of lobster and crab.

Remember that the buffet style of service was invented by Louis XIV, the Sun King! One of life's greatest stylists, Louis loved to fill his solid-gold plate, as he walked along the great trestle tables laden with fresh

Buffet *magnifique* aboard the S.S. *Oceanic* (Home Lines, Inc.).

fruits, appealing appetizers and entrées and rich desserts, sampling as he went.

Chances are there will be a snack bar at the pool, for those who are wearing bathing suits and do not wish to change for the dining salon. Hamburgers, hot dogs, and other sandwiches are available, as well as cold drinks and ice cream.

On some ships, box lunches can be ordered a day ahead from the maitre d' if you are going on a day tour or to the beach while in port. You will find these lunches both delicious and ample: meat or cheese sandwiches, hard-boiled eggs, fruit, and a pastry.

Afternoon tea

Many of the men and women passengers add this friendly afternoon pick-me-up to their daily schedule. Besides tea and coffee, assorted cakes and cookies are served. If you are a health enthusiast and do not take stimulants, ask for "cambric tea" (hot water with lemon or cream). You'll find it very restorative. Many ships also provide soft live music during this restful interlude.

Midnight buffet

This is the fun meal of the day. After returning from a nightclub tour on shore or from dancing beyond limit in the Grand Salon, join your friends in the dining room. The buffet here offers a full meal, desserts, fresh fruit, or cheese and crackers. It's a wonderful time to re-live the day's events, or make plans for the next.

Extra snacks

You may not believe this, but in addition to the lavish meals that have been scheduled by your ship, you'll be looking for still more food in other places. You'll rummage in the fruit basket which the steward places in your cabin every evening (except on the first and last

The Dining Room

nights out), and those food baskets, gifts from your bon voyage party. You'll sneak into the duty free shop onboard ship and buy those pretty French and Swiss chocolates. You'll smuggle aboard all kinds of treats native to the ports your ship visits. And yet, because you've become a perpetual motion machine on this cruise, you may not gain weight but if you should put on a few pounds, treat yourself to a comfortable, flowing caftan or a dashiki. Postpone that diet until you get home.

Typical menus
The ship's purchasing agent garners prize food and drink from around the world and stores it in giant freezers and lockers in the ship's hold.

If your ship specializes in the ethnic dishes of a certain country, be prepared for a delicious adventure.

An outstanding continental cuisine that features Russian specialties is offered aboard March Shipping Corporation cruises.

You'd be surprised how much you can learn about a country simply by eating its native foods.

Most ships offer special menus—and portions—for children, who often prefer a hamburger, peanut-butter sandwiches, or spaghetti to more sophisticated cuisine.

If an American holiday, such as Thanksgiving, occurs while you are onboard ship, rest assured that no matter what flag the ship flies, the chef will turn out a roast turkey with all the trimmings for his Yankee passengers!

Wines

You will enjoy free champagne or cocktails at the Captain's Welcome Aboard Cocktail Party and his Farewell Cocktail Party. Wine, beer, and other alcoholic beverages are also served in the cocktail lounges, at poolside, and in the dining room. These drinks are one of the few items not included in your fare. I suggest you keep a running tab and pay the total bill at the end of your cruise.

The wine steward (*sommelier*, in France) will introduce himself to you at the start of the journey and describe the ship's wine cellar. If you are not a wine expert, let him advise you. If you do not like the wine he recommends, ask him to bring another. Many ships now carry an assortment of wines from the United States as well as choice European vintages.

If you wish to study shipboard prices for wines and other alcoholic beverages, ask the shipping line to mail you their list in advance.

Dining room decorating

Your ship's dining room has been designed to be one of the most inviting places on the ship. Besides the snowy white tablecloths, the sparkling glassware and the bouquets of flowers, you will find glittering ice sculptures on the midnight buffet tables, or perhaps dainty

The Dining Room

baskets woven from strips of chocolate, and filled with bonbons. Sometimes a gala holiday or a seasonal theme highlights the decorations.

Stewards

The foreign stewards and stewardesses on your ship are far from their native land. Many come from countries more family-oriented than ours. They will fuss over your children, fetch high chairs and toys for the little ones and save favorite desserts for the older ones. After all, they miss their own children and parents.

If you are along in years, these efficient and courteous waiters will treat you with a special respect and care, for again, you are the only family they have during most of the year!

The dining room service is impeccable and is like none other on land. You are served in a fashion that you have always hoped for in our hotels but has long vanished. The stewards pamper you shamelessly!

The dining room captains may find out your food preferences and whip up special dishes at your table in their shining chafing dishes, perhaps a Fettucine Alfredo or Crêpes Suzette!

I've never met a steward I didn't like. Nor have I ever met one who wasn't proud of his job and good at it!

The captain's table

Each evening a few passengers are invited to dine at the captain's table. This is a privilege that many prize as highly as an invitation to the White House or a 50-yard line seat at the Rose Bowl game. The shipping line prepares a "Commend List" which usually determines before sailing time who will dine with the captain. I never have been able to figure out just how the main office decides who the captain shall invite—probably by culling the passenger list for celebrities, tycoons, and passengers who have repeated the cruise several times. Don't be surprised, though, if winning first prize at the costume ball or being Mr. or Ms. Congeniality throughout the voyage secures you a place at his table!—the captain may invite whomever he pleases as well as those on the list, for he is truly king of his ship.

The Captain's Farewell Dinner

There will be many gala dinners during the course of your cruise, but the Captain's Farewell Dinner will probably be the most memorable of all.

That afternoon the beauty salon and the barber shop will have plenty of business. The safety deposit boxes in the purser's office will be emptied of their most elaborate jewelry. Men who felt sheepish back home about wearing their floral dinner jackets will don them eagerly. And the women will have found the right occasion for that very becoming and expensive evening dress they just happened to have found that morning in port!

When the passengers parade to their tables, they will find the dining room looking more attractive than ever—glamorous is the word! Sometimes strolling musicians are there to serenade them. Passengers greet the beaming captain with a round of applause to show their admiration and gratitude for his having steered this floating city around the Seven Seas and back to home port.

Sometimes the dining room is likely to be decorated with balloons or garlands. Funny hats and noise makers will be found at each place.

Each course of the meal will be specially selected. Just before dessert time, the lights of the dining room are dimmed, the musicians roll the drums and from the pantry come marching (in military fashion) all the stewards bearing silver trays of baked Alaska or perhaps a flaming dessert.

The Dining Room

Later, when coffee and liqueurs are being savored, the ship's hostess escorts the chief chef, in his immaculate white uniform and tall hat, from table to table, where he receives the plaudits and thanks of the passengers for the superb meals he has prepared for them during the voyage. Some ladies offer him flowers from their table, and some jump up and kiss him. At this point, one of the jubilant passengers usually starts a congo line. Next thing you know everyone is joining in, and the Captain's Farewell Dinner ends with music and laughter and singing.

Tablemates
The Captain's Farewell Dinner is the last time you will be formally seated with your table companions. Many lasting friendships will have been made among those who have shared the same table.

After the Farewell Dinner
After you and your tablemates have exchanged addresses and hugs and kisses, it's time for dancing interspersed with live entertainment in the grand salon. As you climb the stairs, groaning with the pleasures of the meal, you realize with horror balanced by happy anticipation that in only three more hours, you're due back in the dining room for the last Midnight Buffet!

4

Cruise Clothes: Getting All Decked Out

One of the advantages of cruising is the unlimited amount of luggage you may take aboard. If you are leaving from a chilly climate to cruise in a similar environment, you will want to bring warm clothes. In this case, choose your travel clothes so they aren't too bulky to fit into your cabin closet. (There are also hooks on the bulkheads in your cabin but their capacity is limited.) I wear a parka in Alaska, but I have seen many passengers go ashore with just a wind breaker or a raincoat, and they seemed comfortable. (Perhaps my blood has gotten thin after sailing for so many years in the tropics.) You will want to be dressed in a casual way when you are in Alaska. Some of the streets there are unpaved or at best wooden slats with spaces between that catch high heels.

Remember that you will probably be on your feet more than usual during a cruise and select your foot-

THE COMPLETE GUIDE TO A SUCCESSFUL CRUISE

A friend admires Jeraldine's "going-ashore" outfit at the dock in Hains, Alaska.

wear accordingly. Before you sail, make an intensive search for comfortable walking shoes, and attractive but comfortable dancing shoes. And break them in before you embark.

When we're sailing in the tropics, I always keep a plastic bag—the kind that the cleaner slips over your clothes—in my "going-ashore purse." I've found these bags provide sufficient protection during those brief but heavy tropical rainstorms. They are so much lighter and easier to carry than raincoats and can be tossed into the nearest trash bin when the skies have cleared. You might use the plastic bags in place of tissue paper between the folds of your clothes when you're packing.

Cruise Clothes

If you are going to cruise in tropical climes—the Mexican Riviera, the Caribbean, the South Pacific, for example—you won't have to worry about any overweight baggage problems on your flight to where you will board your cruise ship, since you will be carrying lightweight clothing. Women will want to pack a shawl, perhaps, to wear on board in case the air conditioning is too cool at times. And shawls are so flattering—no wonder they're "the look" these days. Such a beautiful selection of colors and patterns are available.

Select a wardrobe that is comfortable and easy to launder. Today's passengers are fortunate in finding a vast array of synthetic drip-dry or naturally crinkly cottons that require no ironing. Just hang them in your shower. Be sure to pack a few of those inflatable rubber hangers that not only speed up the drying but also prevent wrinkles from forming.

You will find no dress code on shipboard, but you will be asked not to wear bathing suits in the dining room and other public rooms. The one essential item, then, is a beach robe or cover-up for jaunts between your cabin and the pool. Your choice can range from loose terry tent dresses to gauzy cottons to long tunics.

On sailing night and last night out (unless the last night is on a three-day cruise), it is not customary to "dress" for dinner. Passengers wear their embarkation clothes on these nights.

When the sun goes down

You will find suggestions for the proper mode of dress in the ship's daily program. Look for these two important events: *Captain's Welcome Aboard Cocktail Party and Dinner* and *Captain's Farewell Dinner*.

These are the two nights—no matter how long or short the cruise—that always require formal attire. Men who do not wish to bring formal dress clothes will not be alone. I've found that only half of the male passengers wear dinner jackets on these nights; the others simply wear suits and ties. Women may choose either long dresses or short cocktail dresses. Either is appropriate.

If you have a favorite outfit, do wear it to the Captain's Welcome Aboard night because that is when the hostess will introduce all the passengers one at a time to the captain. While you are chatting with him your picture will be taken by the ship's photographer. (I can remember, as a cruise hostess, trying to introduce the passengers to the captain and at the same time reminding them to be sure to face the camera because they weren't aware their picture was being taken.)

Here's a hint for the Captain's Farewell Dinner. Make your beauty parlor reservations the first night out. Because passengers are eager to look especially well-groomed on this night the beauty parlor might well be completely booked up, if you don't act early.

On a long cruise—two weeks or more—there may be other nights that are formal. Cruise ships are one of the last places where you still have the opportunity to dress glamorously. It's fun and exciting and can introduce you to a "new" you!

Dinner at Sea we call it when the ship is not in port, and it is not a formal night. On these nights, men may wear a tailored jacket, either matching or contrasting with their trousers, colored shirt and tie or ascot. Dressy pantsuits, floats, or short dresses are appropriate for women.

In Port. When dining on board in port, you are encouraged to dress "casually." Men may wear *guayaberas* (a "must have" for Mexico). This shirt is worn outside the trousers and is an acceptable substitute for the sports jacket and shirt. These well-tailored garments (now available in drip-dry fabrics) have four pockets, originally used for stashing guavas. They can

Cruise Clothes

Captain Piero Buatier and Jeraldine greet this handsome family during the Captain's Welcome Aboard Party on board the *Carla "C."*

be bought in the shop of a Mexico-bound ship or ashore in Mexico and in South America as well. The *barong*, the traditional shirt of the Philippines, is also suitable for dining when the ship is in port. It is similar to the *guayaberas*, and either may be worn with aplomb to the fanciest restaurant when going ashore in the tropics. Another very "in" look is the *aloha* shirt—and not just in Hawaii.

If the ship is in a colder climate and you are dining onboard in port, a sport shirt or sweater will be fine.

In other words, you always dress "casually" in the dining room while the ship is in port. The ladies wear sun dresses or pants with colorful tops. Sweaters and skirts, even blue jeans, are worn in colder climates on *In-Port* nights.

Caftans, floats, and blousons are my favorite attire for dining both in port or at sea. Big, over-sized smock tops have a newer silhouette to them than T-shirts and halters, and pants are more fashionable if they are simply straight-cut. The idea is to have plenty of room at the top of your oufit and less below.

I'm sure you will be buying clothes in the ship's shop during your cruise, so don't worry if you haven't the time or can't just find the outfit that would be indigenous to the ports to which you are sailing. Part of the fun of cruising is shopping on board and in the ports.

During the day, on board ship, anything goes. For the deck you will want sun hats, scarves, shorts, slacks, bathing suits, sun dresses, skirts, and tops. Don't worry about your daytime clothes. Let them be comfortable and easy, and you'll feel that way too.

For evening, let yourself go in any direction you'd like: sleek and sophisticated, feminine and romantic, sultry, mysterious—whatever you'd like to be. It's pretend time. Be whoever you've always wanted to be, for nighttime on shipboard is a chance to get "all decked out."

To summarize:

Formal dress means dinner jacket or suit and tie; Long or short evening gown or other dressy outfit.

Informal dress means a business suit or sports jacket and slacks with tie or ascot; Regular dress, cocktail dress, pantsuit, or sports outfit.

Casual dress means sports shirt and slacks, sports outfit (no tie); Sun dress, skirt and blouse, and even blue jeans and sweaters.

5

Let Us Entertain You

*A little nonsense now and then
is relished by the wisest men.*

—Anonymous

One of the most-often asked questions by those who have not sailed on a cruise ship is, "What do people do all day out there on the ocean?"

A curious truth about cruising is that the days seem to melt into one another. And, as the cruise progresses, the days feel as though they are getting increasingly shorter.

In other words, there is so much happening onboard that time passes with the speed of summer lightning. There are interesting activities for everyone at all times of the day.

It is smart to remember to become involved in at least some of the activities since it is the most natural way of meeting new friends. Entertainment on board ship is arranged in a well-balanced daily program by the cruise director and his staff.

THE COMPLETE GUIDE TO A SUCCESSFUL CRUISE

On the shuffle board courts aboard Holland America's S.S. *Rotterdam*.

Most cruise ships carry a bridge lecturer, and some ships are officially sanctioned by the American Contract Bridge League, so passengers may earn Master Points while on board. And remember, one of the cardinal rules of cruising is to be sure to read the day's events published every day in the cruise director's daily program. In this way, you will avoid missing activities that may have special appeal for you.

Let Us Entertain You

Deck games in session on one of the sports decks aboard the S.S. *Statendam*.

On the open decks, games such as deck tennis, Ping-Pong, shuffleboard and trapshooting are common. You might wish to join a jogging group or a walkathon. And, of course, there will be a swimming pool for swimming and sun-bathing.

Boards for chess, backgammon, and scrabble are also available. There is usually a library and a quiet room for reading and writing.

THE COMPLETE GUIDE TO A SUCCESSFUL CRUISE

Tennis lessons aboard the M.S. *Caribe*, Commodore Cruise Line Ltd.

Skeet shooting on the S.S. *Doric*, Home Lines, Inc.

Let Us Entertain You

Golf on board the *Monarch Sun*.

THE COMPLETE GUIDE TO A SUCCESSFUL CRUISE

There's ample space aft for sun-worshippers aboard the *Golden Odyssey*, Royal Cruise Line.

Let Us Entertain You

THE COMPLETE GUIDE TO A SUCCESSFUL CRUISE

The Lido Sun Deck on the *Emerald Seas*, Eastern Steamship Lines, Inc.

Poolside activities on board a Sitmar cruise.

Let Us Entertain You

A quiet moment in the library on a Sitmar Line cruise.

S.S. *Oceanic*'s reading and writing room. (Home Lines, Inc.)

THE COMPLETE GUIDE TO A SUCCESSFUL CRUISE

There are theme cruises with enrichment lectures you may want to hear. Giving lectures on cruise ships—and writing—are now my life's work. I sail on various cruise lines and when I do, the lines call them "Love Boat Cruises." So you may find me on one of your cruises lecturing on my favorite subjects, such as "Vim and Vigor," nutrition, and astrology.

There's sure to be a morning exercise class in the gym, if your ship has one, or on deck, if not. You're

The charm of the *Carnivale* and the *Mardi Gras* cruise ships is the versatility of life on board during the seven-day cruises with an all-Italian crew! Here you see a bit of the action at a casino on board.

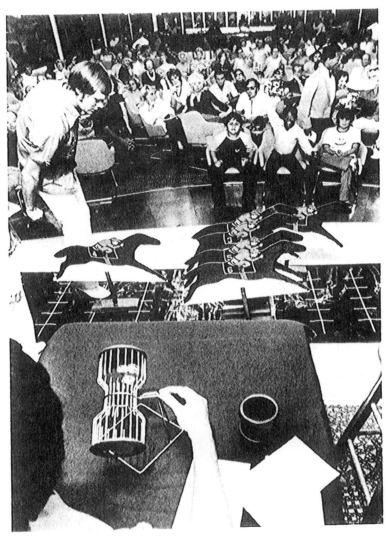
Horseracing on the Norwegian Caribbean Line.

likely to find a dance class, too, taught by professional dance instructors.

And twelve miles out to sea gambling is legal! You can play bingo, horse racing (played with wooden horses and dice), or you can place a wager on the ship's daily run, which is called the mileage pool. Some ships have gambling tables with dealers—a bit of Las Vegas! These tables are busy until the wee hours of the morning. And slot machines, of course!

Depending on the size of the ship, there'll be at least two or three orchestras on board for dancing.

Current movies you'll find, too, as well as interesting travel films; the latter are usually shown during the morning or just before lunchtime.

Every night the ship is at sea professional entertainment is offered in one of the main lounges or the nightclub. These variety-type shows usually last about an hour. Ladies need no escort for these shows. It's like one big private party.

If you really want to be alone on the cruise to settle in a deck chair and gulp in that heavenly sea air, nobody is going to bother you. But if you want to be part of the gang and enjoy "Show Business on the High Seas," you may see anything from a high-spirited amateur crew show to guest appearances by Broadway and television personalities.

Your cruise director is always an experienced master of ceremonies, often with an act of his own as a comic, a singer, or a dancer. The ship's hostess and other cruise staff members also are chosen to make their moments in the spotlight count.

The orchestras will make every effort to play the kind of music YOU like to dance to, whether it's a Lawrence Welk smoothie or a Future Shock Rock for the trendy.

The grand salon (sometimes called the main ballroom or main salon) is the location for the really big shows. The nightclub is used as a discotheque and for more intimate reviews.

You may enjoy a cooking demonstration stirred up by a globetrotting gourmet or by the ship's chef in the dining room. In fine weather, a stunning torchlit tropical show may be presented by the pool.

Let Us Entertain You

Continental Lounge aboard the S.S. *Doric*, Home Lines, Inc.

Show Time can be any hour and *anywhere* on board ship.

Your entertainment may be geared to give you a cultural taste of the ports of call. On Mexican cruises, we usually feature dancers from the spectacular Ballet Folklorico of Mexico City and mariachi bands from all over the land of *mucho gusto*. Heading for the Caribbean, we offer you ruffle-shirted Calypso singers and agile Limbo dancers who slither under poles placed lower and lower and show *you* how to do it too. In the South Seas, every island will perform their special dances for you on board ship.

Occasionally a business or club will organize a group and sail together. Some are so large they will book an entire ship. Then the shows presented will be tailored to the group's wishes. It's a wonderful way to zero in on a particular subject. I remember some very progressive convention shows, lectures, and panel discussions conducted on board on topics such as aging, preventive medicine, and parapsychology. If the group hasn't booked the whole ship, the activities are held in separate areas.

A "crew show" on board a Sun Line cruise.

Let Us Entertain You

W.F. and R.K. Swan (Hellenic) Ltd. (Esplanade Tours, Boston, Massachusetts). One of the most exotic cruises is offered by the M.S. *Delta* which sails the Nile. The M.T.S. *Orpheus*, built in Ireland with the highest safety classification of Lloyd's of London, tours the Mediterranean. Here Jeraldine joins in the Greek dancing on board the *Orpheus*.

On a long cruise, when you spend many nights at sea between ports, the cruise director will have a great variety of shows to keep you amused.

If your ship is staffed with personnel from a country famous for its folk music and dances, there may be a Crew Show. It is thrilling to see them, dressed in the costumes of their native land, tossing off high notes and kicking up their heels!

THE COMPLETE GUIDE TO A SUCCESSFUL CRUISE

There may be a Passenger Show. On a long cruise, the cruise director and the orchestra leader will audition the passengers and help those who have specific talents put on a show. You'll cheer and whistle for the quiet girl at your table who turns out to be a sizzling belly dancer and the salesman who plays the Warsaw Concerto like Liberace!

Water games on board Costa Line's *Italia*.

Let Us Entertain You

On a long cruise, there'll be a night of unique shipboard games that delight and are conducive to "letting your hair down," plus parlor games—all the hilarious oldies but goodies. You'll find out everyone on board gets a kick out of these participation games and that your fellow passengers love to be playful.

There may be a Champagne Night. This is the night when the hardworking dance instructors proudly trot out their protegés. There has been an afternoon rehearsal, and special instructions about how to zig instead of zag if the ship tilts in a heavy sea.

Some of the memorable passenger dance teams I remember are the silver-haired couples, the ladies beautiful in chiffon, floating through the *Anniversary Waltz*.

Others have been just as memorable:

A Brazilian siren in tight satin, doing a Latin medley with her Valentino-like husband.

A bald, heavy set businessman who did a wild jitterbug with his teeny-bopper daughter.

A black model with a fantastic figure doing a boogaloo with our dance instructor. They couldn't be outclassed by any Las Vegas floor show!

A group of fun-loving middle-aged housewives doing a Charleston line that brought the house down!

When it came time for the judges to award the champagne prizes, these were all winners!

Island Night, if you are cruising the South Seas, is when every passenger turns native. Leis, lava lavas, and love permeate the atmosphere. Passengers become nature's children.

The Costume Ball

When your travel agent mentions the Costume Ball, you'll probably groan, "You mean I have to take a bulky costume to use just once?" Never fear, you have many options.

THE COMPLETE GUIDE TO A SUCCESSFUL CRUISE

1. Don't participate. Be a spectator. If the Grand Salon doesn't have applauding admirers, where's the fun for the contestants? (The cruise director always hopes that half the passengers will make up the audience and half will join in the parade.)

2. Go to the rummage-table set up by the cruise staff on the day of the ball. You'll find various things, perhaps crepe paper, funny hats, artificial flowers, pins, string, tape, and other items, and the staff will also help you create a spur-of-the-moment costume.

3. Join a creative group. For example, you could come as the Carter Family: a Bible for Miss Lillian, a beer can for Billy, and lovable grins and bags of peanuts for everyone else.

4. Decide you're out to win the "most-beautiful" category! Before you sail, sew, borrow, rent, or buy the most fabulous costume you can find!

The lineup

After dinner on the night of the ball, the cruise staff organizes the Costume Parade. The hostess usually signs the contestants in. It's easy for her to recognize characters like King Kong or Cleopatra, but don't be disappointed, should you be wearing a flour sack with a thermometer taped to your forehead, if she doesn't instantly write down "Miss Pillsbury Bake-Off"! And please don't expect her to recognize you if you're dressed in your outlandish garb.

Children in the parade usually go first so they can be sent off to their bunks early.

The cruise director appoints judges at random from the audience. They are the ones who will choose the "Most Beautiful," "Most Original," "Funniest," etc., while the parade goes on.

The orchestra gives a fanfare, the cruise director takes over the hostess's list, and the costume parade begins. The cruise director calls out, "Mary Smith as

Carmen!" and the contestant steps out into the spotlight as the orchestra plays an appropriate tune such as "Lady of Spain." Then she moves on to march around the dance floor while the next contestant steps into the spotlight.

Once in a while, the contestant's get-up is so hilariously funny, the cruise director will stop the music and exchange a few jokes. But usually the line-up is so long that the parade is kept moving at a good pace.

Typical costumes

There are certain costumes that always seem to turn up in every parade. For instance, the girl with the most divine figure always wears a revealing bikini, and the girl with the worst figure also wears a revealing bikini. They may wear a banner "Miss SS Queen Mary" or whatever the name of the ship is on which they are sailing.

There's always one couple where the rugged looking husband dresses like a woman and his beautiful wife dresses like a man. This is always good for lots of laughs!

There's the Tourist Lady who piles a dozen sun hats on her head, loads herself down with shopping bags stuffed with souvenirs, slaps sun block on her burned nose, and wraps her aching feet in Dr. Scholl's Footpads. She always gets a sympathetic hand.

I've seen a few go through the parade more than once, taking off more and more of their costumes each time. We had our share of stripteasers, "streakers," and "flashers."

My suggestion: the costumes that go over the best (and are usually the winners) are the ones *obviously* made on board. It is amazing what a little creativity can do with the bits and pieces provided by cruise staff on the afternoon of costume night.

Some of the authentic foreign costumes can be lovely,

A cruise to Canada and Alaska will afford you magnificent views of majestic mountains and "free form" icebergs, sculptured by the tireless wind and water.

Let Us Entertain You

and some of the original designs really far-out (like the computer man with flashing lights from a built-in battery).

The most spectacular costume I have ever seen onboard ship was not part of the contest. We always save it for the finale of the parade. It is the God of the Feathered Serpent designed by Eduardo Rivera, one of the dancers from the Ballet Folklorico. His bronze body, covered with only a gold loincloth and a bib of gold and jewels, is outlined in a flowing cape of many colors and a towering headdress of gold and feathers. He really looks like a god come to earth in this costume.

The greatest shows are often seen on the water and totally unplanned. You might see a school of whales that may surface alongside the ship, or a leaping porpoise. And there is the ever-present spectacular ice-show to be viewed from the deck of ships exploring Alaska or the Norwegian fjords.

Life on board ship is everything but dull! Everything is directed to make you welcome, keep you happy, and for your entertainment.

6

Ports of Call

Although the ports of call are usually the first thing looked at when you check through the travel brochures, you will find the ports take second place in interest after you've taken your cruise. This is because the ship and the great time you've had on it will remain uppermost in your memory.

A travel agency is the best place to go for any and all help when making decisions about taking a cruise. There is no fee for this service because the cruise lines and air lines pay the travel agencies. Their help is immeasurable; you might as well let them do all the phoning, planning, and worrying for you. Because they are such travel lovers they know how to help you get the most for your money.

Tip: If you are trying to book a cruise which is already full, the travel agent can place you on a waiting list. No use going to another travel agent to get on

THE COMPLETE GUIDE TO A SUCCESSFUL CRUISE

The magnificent M.S. *Golden Odyssey* anchored in the charming port of Hydra, the midway point of one of her summer "Seas of Ulysses" Mediterranean air/sea cruises.

their waiting list also because there is only one list which all agents use and that is at the cruise line's office so it won't help any to have more than one agent put you on this list.

It is usually best to try to arrange for a cruise that is in port during a weekday, if it is a port where you want to shop. Naturally, you will be in some ports on Sundays and that is fun, too, because the ship will help you to get on a tour of each and every port.

I highly recommend taking the ship-arranged tour in every port that you haven't visited before. Ship tours

Ports of Call

take you quickly and efficiently to all the most noteworthy places in or near the port. After you have had lunch or dinner on the ship, there is often time to go ashore again for a more leisurely inspection of places that caught your fancy.

If your ship is not docked but at anchor, the tenders will take you back and forth from the ship to the dock.

By transiting the Panama Canal you can cruise through two oceans, two worlds! As you cross between the Caribbean and the Pacific through the great Canal Locks, a special guide will point out the marvels of this engineering feat.

These tenders usually go every 20 to 30 minutes and there is no charge. Women should bring a scarf for their hair, since some tenders don't have tops. I suggest you bring (or buy in the first port) a large straw bag to use as a purse and for carrying your shopping treasures.

Some ship tours are limited in the number of passengers they can take because in some ports there are a limited number of taxis or buses available.

Some passengers are quick to say, "I hate tours." They miss the point. Most cruise ships are in port for only a short time, one or two days, and if it is your first time there, you'll want to see the most interesting attractions. If you try to find them for yourself, that is perfectly fine, but I know the pitfalls of going this way. Drivers not affiliated with the tour, may, and often do, take you to their Uncle Joe's combination general-store-and-café or to the stores of friends and relatives. And even if you have an understanding with the driver about his charges, he may charge you more than he said he would. This is not always the case, of course, but I have heard so many passengers complain about this practice that I feel I must mention it.

Although shore excursion tickets are sold on the ship, these tours are usually owned and operated by an outside company. Sometimes there are several different excursions offered for each port. This is why it is so necessary to attend the port lecture given by the cruise director the day before the ship arrives in that port. These port talks are most informative. A brief history of the port is given, local points of interest are described, and shopping hints are provided. Be sure to bring pen and paper for notes.

Shore excursions include: city tours, beach parties, shopping tours, nightclub tours, and last, but not least, if in Mexico—the fabulous fiestas!

7

Traveling Unattached

Tied to the dock, the Love Boat can't sail,
If she stayed that way, there'd be no tale.
"Let go all lines—Get underway"
These are the words her Captain must say
If she is to leave port and make to sea
Carrying all on board to their destiny.
Learn from the Love Boats your "Lesson One,"
Tied to the dock, naught can be done.
"Let go all lines" that hold you fast,
"Get underway" and find joy at last.
Let the Love Boats show you the way,
Life needs not be a bore, but a happy holiday.

—Arthur Andrews

Cruise ships have some activities that are strictly for singles. This doesn't mean that you must be single, it just means you must be traveling alone, unattached for the time being. For you, the most important event of the whole cruise will be the Singles Party. It's the greatest opportunity you'll have to meet others who are also traveling alone.

The party will be announced in your daily program—usually the second or third night out. It's generally a cocktail party, starting about 6:00 P.M. Sometimes the captain and the officers join the guests, if it is a day when they are not busy with ship's duties.

THE COMPLETE GUIDE TO A SUCCESSFUL CRUISE

Romance is for all ages on the Holland American Line's Monarch cruises.

All the ship's entertainers and cruise staff attend, and it is really a very special time. In fact, usually one staff member must be stationed at the door to keep envious couples from trying to "crash" the party.

This may be your only chance to find out who else is traveling unattached. So remember, if you're "sailing solo," make it a must on your list of things to do. You'll find that there are many people, besides yourself, who are eager to find companionship.

To get the most out of life, we must reach out to one another, and shipboard is the perfect place to find the innate warmth that all humans possess.

8

Cruise Etiquette

It is something to be able to paint a particular picture, or to carve a statue, and so to make a few objects beautiful, but it is far more glorious to carve and paint the very atmosphere and medium through which we look—to affect the quality of the day—that is the highest of arts.
—Henry Thoreau

Let's face it, when you decided to go on the cruise, you signed up for a good time, and you will get much more than you bargained for—more than luxurious surroundings and heavenly meals—if you have the correct attitude.

You will appreciate the easy familiarity and informal atmosphere of friendliness among your fellow passengers and crew. Introductions are not necessary aboard ship. Passengers introduce themselves to each other as though they were at a private party. Of course, you won't force yourself on fellow passengers but you can smile, nod, or say hello as you wish. One of the most remarkable things about cruising is the pervasive enthusiasm and all-embracing goodwill that it promotes.

The brilliant writer, M.F.K. Fisher, in her book, *The Gastronomical Me*, remarks that people who travel by

THE COMPLETE GUIDE TO A SUCCESSFUL CRUISE

Jeraldine introduces passengers to the captain aboard Costa Line's *Carla "C."*

water experience a mystical "sea change" each time they board a seagoing ship.

When you travel for pleasure, have an attitude that is flexible and sensitive and tactful. This attitude will pass travel etiquette requirements everywhere. Of all the qualities that make Americans likeable, none is greater than tact, the quick awareness and consideration of the feelings of others. (One can be very sincere and still be tactful.)

Cruising is the perfect place to reap the profits and advantages of good manners. When in doubt as to what is "correct," follow your kind impulses. For etiquette is decency, ethical integrity and self-respect creating an atmosphere that makes it pleasant for others to be near you. Your etiquette colors your day. To repeat what Thoreau said: " . . . to affect the quality of the day—that is the highest of arts."

9

Vim and Vigor: Health Tips For Cruise Passengers

*Joy and temperance and repose
Slam the door on the doctor's nose.*
—Longfellow

Because you will want to feel tip-top during every moment of your cruise, I am going to tell you how to avoid those things that could hinder your enjoying life to the fullest while sailing.

Remember to pack any regular medications you must take. Don't count on your prescriptions being filled in the ship infirmary. Each cruise ship that goes more than 2½ hours from shore has a doctor on board and a hospital. These hospitals are for emergencies; they are not there to sell drugs.

Passengers sometimes complain of swollen feet or ankles. This may be because they are eating more desserts than usual or perhaps drinking more coffee, which is also a burden on the kidneys. Moderation may avoid this. *Natural* Vitamin C, nature's own diuretic, is a good item to pack in your medicine kit.

Be sure to ask your travel agent if you will need any shots for the particular cruise you are taking. Often none are necessary. If you must have shots, make arrangements to get them as far ahead of sailing time as possible—just in case you have a reaction. If you wear glasses, bring an extra pair along.

It is a good idea to have your teeth checked to avoid any surprise flare-ups in that department!

Travel by ship usually eliminates the worry of getting the "touristas" (dysentery) because you will be eating your meals on board. But it is interesting to eat ashore occasionally or at least have a drink so I will give you some rules that will help prevent dysentery.

In ports where the water is known to "not agree" with tourists, the best hotels have their own water purifying equipment. In roadside cafés in these ports, it is best to drink only bottled water. If the café is one you are not sure of, don't order anything with ice cubes!

If you plan on eating in a restaurant in a port that is known for its "touristas," or "Montezuma's Revenge," a good preventive medication to take just before you eat is *Entero Via Forma*. This can be purchased in pharmacies in Mexico without a prescription, and it has been found most effective by many.

If you have already come down with dysentery, it is too late for *Entero Via Forma*. In this case, you should take *Lomotil*, which also can be purchased in most drug stores in Mexico without a prescription. It is a good idea to take yogurt tablets each time you take one of these medicines. But it's even better, if you like yogurt, to eat it regularly before and during your cruise. Yogurt discourages the growth of pathogenic organisms. If you don't like the taste of yogurt, just take the yogurt tablets daily. Milk may not be safe in some ports, but yogurt is safe everywhere because of its ability to destroy bacteria. Please don't get the yogurt sweetened with sugar. Sugar is not only fatten-

Vim and Vigor

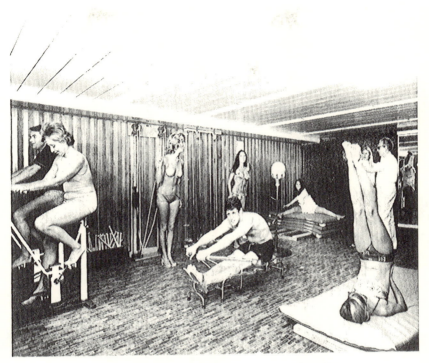

Getting in shape on board the S.S. *Doric*, Home Lines, Inc.

ing, but is toxic and draws nutrients *from* your body to be able to digest it. To keep from being bitten by insects, many people take Vitamin B.

Most passengers on cruises don't get seasick, but some are prone to seasickness. Here's how to avoid it. On days when there is a rough sea, take one Dramamine tablet right away. If you wait until you feel seasick, the tablet may not stay down. If you are regurgitating because you didn't take your Dramamine in time, you can always ask the ship's doctor to give you a Dramamine suppository or a Dramamine shot.

It is possible to avoid all this even though you are prone to motion sickness. If the sea is smooth, but a warning is out that a storm lies ahead, there will be time to put food in your stomach before the storm starts. If it's between-meals when you hear the warning you can always ask the bartender for some peanuts or order something from room service. The secret is to eat *before* you feel "queezy." Then you probably won't need the Dramamine because having some food digesting in your stomach is even more effective in preventing seasickness.

Two important things to remember on those rare days when the seas are rough and you want to make sure you won't be seasick: Do not drink liquids of any kind. This includes coffee (especially), soups, Cokes, 7-Up, etc. Have some solid foods in your stomach at all times.

If you follow these two rules, no matter how sensitive to motion you are, there is a good chance you will be able to take the roughest seas just like an "old salt."

One of the best sunburn preventives is Sea and Ski. It's also good to use after being in the sun to keep your skin from peeling. But do be careful about the length of time you stay in the sun the first few days. Remember, you get a double-dose when you're aboard ship, for the sea reflects the sun much more powerfully than land.

Fatigue can also waste some of your precious cruise hours. To get the most from your vacation and to sustain a feeling of well-being, it is wise to take an "all-in-one" vitamin tablet plus a Vitamin B Complex and a natural Vitamin C tablet with each meal. The B will help you sleep well and provide you with extra energy, while C will help prevent infections and colds.

If you are wise in selecting your choice of foods on board, a cruise can be a health-giving experience. Even the bread, although usually made from white flour, is more nutritious because it is baked fresh every day and, therefore, no chemical additives are needed to store it.

Vim and Vigor

Jogging on the decks on a Sun Line cruise.

The two main culprits for draining energy are refined sugar and caffeine, and any foods or drinks containing them. They give you a quick pickup which leaves you, an hour or two later, feeling lower than you felt before. And later the caffeine makes acid in your stomach which makes you crave more food than you would want otherwise. Refined sugar is an empty food that just goes to fat.

One last suggestion for traveler's health. I suggest you bring along alfalfa tablets (available in health food stores) if you are prone to constipation. Take three or four tablets after each meal. Besides relieving constipation, they will add valuable nutrients to your diet.

Before you leave home, study nutrition, learn how to select your food wisely. You'll be surprised at how much vim and vigor you'll have for your cruise activities!

10

The Art of Traveling

Travel expectantly.
Every place you visit
is like a surprise package
to be opened.
Untie the strings
with an expectation
of high adventure.

Travel with curiosity.
It is not how far you go,
but how deeply you do
that mines the gold
of experience.

Travel with imagination.
As the old Spanish proverb puts it:
"He who would bring home
the wealth of the Indies
must carry
the wealth of
the Indies with him."

THE COMPLETE GUIDE TO A SUCCESSFUL CRUISE

Travel relaxed.
Make up your mind
to have a good time.
Travel with the spirit
of a world citizen.
You'll discover that people
are basically much the same
the world around.
Be an ambassador of good will
to all people.

—From *The Art of Living*
by Wilfred A. Peterson

11

The Joy of Shopping on the Bounding Main

Shopping is one of the many enticements for taking a cruise. Those who must travel by air from the ship may avoid extra-weight charges by mailing their purchases from home port—or sending them by U.P.S.

Local handicrafts are the most exciting finds in each port.

You readers will be wise shoppers for having studied this book's chapter on U.S. customs. I feel that buying more than your allotted amount and paying the "overage" when going through customs will save you money—even with the tax, if you are a good shopper. Your purchases will undoubtedly be a lot cheaper than if you bought them in the United States, especially if you buy the best buys in each port. (I have many chapters on this in *The Love Boats*, but to summarize: Wise buys are usually what each port is known for. The cruise director and his staff will be helpful here. They

THE COMPLETE GUIDE TO A SUCCESSFUL CRUISE

Shopping arcade aboard the S.S. *Doric,* Home Lines, Inc.

will always be eager to give you any information you want, but rather than having each passenger ask them, "What are the best buys in our next port?" it would be best if all passengers attended the port lecture and jotted down the vital information at that time.

I have found during many years of living on cruise ships and being an avid shopper myself, that some of the best buys can be found right on your ship in the ship's boutique shop.

Shopping on the Bounding Main

The ship's shop is a duty-free center that usually offers a wide variety of gifts, souvenirs, wearing apparel, and other fine merchandise from all over the world. The buyers for these shops get things in ports at costs that are sometimes less than wholesale, so I find the same things on shore sometimes much more expensive. When shopping on board, you aren't limited to just the things that are found in the ports of your particular cruise. You will find there a dazzling profusion of treasures from the world over, and all of them exempt from import tariffs.

Because the ship's shop is duty-free, it must, according to international customs regulations, remain closed while the ship is in port. But you will find the shop open daily while the ship is at sea. These shops also stock film, toilet articles, and other items you may need.

If you buy interesting and unusual objects that are local specialities, you will love your purchases as will the receiver of your gifts. Original art—paintings, sculpture, carvings, and textiles—is especially fine.

12

What to Do If You Find Yourself on the *Leaking Lena*

Most of the cruise liners I have worked on have been super "posh." But just as an actor isn't always on Broadway, I have had some off-Broadway experiences.

And just as a mutt may give you more love than a purebred, I have found that sometimes a *Leaking Lena* can be just as much fun as if it were ship-shape. A few shared "hardships" seem to bring out a bubbling humor in even the dourest passenger. I can truly tell you, even with a Godzilla or two along (See chapter 14) you can sometimes have more fun than if everything is running smoothly. Passengers write poems, songs, and plays for Talent Night dramatizing all the things that have gone wrong.

I spent a six month season on a real tub. This poor ship had trouble in every area, from its defunct hot water tank to missing ports because it couldn't get up enough speed! I can truthfully tell you that because the passengers were determined to enjoy themselves, come hell or high water, they had more fun on this old wreck than they would have had on one of the posh ships. In fact, much to my surprise, each time we sailed, we had a line of repeat passengers ready for another adventurous cruise.

So if you find yourself on a ship that is not your idea of the ultimate, do not despair. You can help turn the cruise into an experience you wouldn't have missed for anything.

Whether your ship is the newest or oldest, biggest or smallest, it is your *attitude* that flavors the success of your cruise.

13

Guidelines on Tipping

It is strictly up to you how much and whom you tip. But one of the first questions passengers ask me is, "When and how and whom am I supposed to tip?" I want to give you some general guidelines, because I promised to save you from any embarrassment.

Although tipping is an individual thing, you will probably want to follow the custom of most cruise passengers. They tip their cabin steward and their dining-room table steward weekly, or, if it is not a long cruise, no longer than seventeen days, they tip at the end of the trip. Others who serve you, in the bars and lounges and on deck, are usually tipped at the time of service, as you would do ashore in a hotel. Gratuities to the maitre d' are in order if he has changed your table, arranged for a private celebration (birthday, anniversary, etc.), or performed some other special service. There is also a head waiter who is in charge of a particular section of the dining room. The tip for the maitre d' and head waiter is completely up to the passenger's discretion. The wine steward usually gets 15% of your wine bill.

How much to tip? Here again it is up to you. It should depend on your appraisal of the attendant's service and friendliness. If you need a rule of thumb (keeping inflation in mind), in 1978 $2.00 per day *per passenger* is about average for the cabin steward, and the same amount for your table steward.

There are envelopes in the purser's office for tips, but I feel it is more gracious to use your own personal envelopes. Please hand the envelope to your cabin and table stewards personally. Do not leave these tips on your dresser or on the table where it could be picked up by the wrong person. If you have more than one table steward, hand it to the one who takes your order. He will share it with his assistant. It is the same with your cabin steward. If he has an assistant, he will share it with him.

Please remember to save enough cash for tips. It can be very difficult for crew members to cash travelers checks and almost impossible for them to cash a personal check.

You will even *enjoy* tipping on board ship because you will have grown so fond of the crew!

14
The Distinctive Language of the Sea

Sailors have always had a colorful language, uniquely theirs. Expressions come from different sources because of the overlapping history of maritime peoples. Words, terms, and phrases describe a hard and demanding life that is steeped in traditions. The following is just a sampling of the words and phrases you may hear on your cruise:

Nautical Terms

Abaft—Toward the stern, or further back than. Starting point can be anywhere. Like "The stern is abaft the bow," or "John is abaft Mary." (*See* Aft.)
Above—Upstairs ("Gone above"). Remember, there are no stairs on a ship. (*See* Companionway.)
Aboveboard—Out in the open, or topside. Perhaps the source of expression for frank, candid.

THE COMPLETE GUIDE TO A SUCCESSFUL CRUISE

Aft—Toward the stern ("Go aft"). The stern is the rear end of the ship.

Alleyway—Passageway or corridor. Doors to the cabins face onto the alleyway.

Amidships—The middle of the ship, halfway between port and starboard. When the ship lays a straight wake, the rudder is amidships.

Anchor—A heavy steel device attached to a chain that is attached to the ship to hold it in place, offshore, when not underway.

Athwartship, Thwartship—Means horizontal, going from side to side rather than fore and aft. A seat in a lifeboat is called a "thwart" because it runs from one side of the boat to the other.

Avast—Don't ask, "A vast what?" Avast means to stop right now. Example, "Avast there, you landlubber."

Ballast—Weight used to keep a ship in trim. Usually carried by unloaded freighters and tankers to keep them from riding high out of the water.

Beam—The widest athwartship dimension of the vessel. "Broad off the beam" means at right angles to the direction of travel of the vessel.

Bell—Not used for passengers, crew only; to tell time by hearing the bells, you must know:

> Two bells is one, five, or nine o'clock.
> Four bells is two, six, or ten o'clock.
> Six bells is three, seven, or eleven o'clock.
> Eight bells is four, eight, or twelve o'clock.
> The half hour is designated by striking the hour, a pause, then one additional strike of the bell.

Also, a signal from bridge to engine room.

Bell buoy—A marker buoy with bell that rings because of wave motion.

Below—Downstairs ("Go below").

Bilge—The bottom part of the ship.

Bitter end—The end of the line (rope).

The Distinctive Language of the Sea

Bitts—Heavy steel posts rising from the deck for securing hawsers, lines, and cables.

Boat drill—An exercise in safety required by law and common sense.

Bow—The front end of the ship; the end that's pointing toward where you are going.

Breastline—This term has nothing to do with fashion, sex, or anatomy! It's just another rope with a specific job. A breastline keeps the ship alongside the dock. There is also the springline and the sternline, which have to do with the forward motion of the ship at dock. The bowline prevents aft motion of the ship at dock.

Bridge—The captain's command post. The center of navigation and technical communications necessary for operating the ship. This is where the helmsman steers the vessel, where the officer of the watch holds forth. Here you will find the compass, the radar screen and other electronic navigational aids.

Bulkhead—Those up-and-down things called "walls" back home.

Bumboat—A small craft, usually a rowboat, from which the natives sell artifacts, handicrafts, and local produce.

Bunk—Your bed aboard ship.

Cabin—Your bedroom, sometimes called a "stateroom."

Cable—A heavy fiber or wire rope, often a chain, used for towing and anchoring.

Capstan—A machine used for hauling in cable. The revolving drum is generally vertical. When it's horizontal, it's called a winch.

Captain—"The Old Man" (this term used only behind his back!), the person in charge of the ship. You, the crew, and the ship are his responsibility. Therefore, at sea, you are under his authority. No wonder he sometimes looks worried. But the appellation "Old Man" does not fit most cruise ship captains, who are usually suave, sophisticated, and handsome, as well as superbly competent at their job.

Carried away—A line, boom, or spar that has broken or yielded under load or strain.

Chart—There are no "maps" aboard ship. All maps are called charts.

Chart room—Where the navigator operates. Charts, notices to mariners, books, and navigational records are kept here.

Chasing the compass—This happens when the order is given to change course, and the helmsman (usually a neophyte) "steers" the compass instead of the ship. This maneuver results in instant-chagrin and instant-learning! If your companion should make a wrong maneuver, you might say he's "chasing the compass."

Chow down—Eating-time aboard ship, a phrase frequently heard on cruise ships.

Coaming—A curb around a hatchway (an opening on deck). Be careful that you do not stumble over one of these.

Companionway—The interior stairway aboard ship.

Compass—The navigational instrument of utmost importance. It always points North, enabling the navigator to direct the ship's course without reference to the sun or stars which may not be visible during a storm or heavy fog.

Crew—The officer's helpers. They carry out the officer's orders just as officers must carry out the captain's orders.

Cruise staff—As far as the passengers are concerned, the cruise staff are among the most important people aboard ship. They are headed by the cruise director. Their total involvement is YOU, your enjoyment, entertainment, and pleasure.

Davits—A pair of devices from which a lifeboat is suspended and which also lowers it and hauls it up from the sea.

Davy Jones' locker—The bottom of the sea.

The Distinctive Language of the Sea

Deadlight—The protective steel porthole used to cover the glass porthole.

Dead reckoning—An educated guess about a ship's position at sea, based only on the compass and the ship's log. To make this computation correctly is the mark of a "born sailor."

Deck—The floor of a ship. For example: Promenade deck, also "A" deck, "B" deck, etc. Actually, there are floors on a ship, but you'll never see them. They are part of the structure of the tanks that form the ship's double bottom.

Deep six—To "deep six it" is to throw something overboard.

Disembark—To get off ship. Unfortunately, you have to when the cruise is over.

Dog—The metal fastening devices used on hatches and doors.

Draft—It is the measure in feet from the waterline to the bottom of the keel, i.e., how deep the ship is riding in the water.

Dressing ship—To display all the ship's signal flags for decorative or communicative purposes.

Embark—To go aboard your cruise ship (one of life's happiest experiences).

Fairway—A passage or open channel, as between two points of land.

Fantail—The part of the stern of a vessel extending abaft the sternpost.

Fathom—A nautical unit, measuring six feet in length. Thirty fathoms of water equals 180 feet.

Fathometer—A navigational device for measuring the depth of water.

Flagstaff—the staff to which the ensign is hoisted. In this case, ensign is a flag and not a junior officer!

Forecastle (Pronounced Fo'c'sle)—The forward part of the ship. Once upon a time it was the crew's quarter. Now, it is generally used for storage. It's the worst place to be when it is stormy and the ship is pitching.

THE COMPLETE GUIDE TO A SUCCESSFUL CRUISE

Forward—Towards the bow ("He's forward"). The term is used to indicate position of something that is closer to the bow than the speaker.

Freshen the nip—To shift a line to take the wear in another place.

Galley—The kitchen of the ship. Your cruise ship will have a main galley and several smaller units called pantries, which are used by the stewards who pamper you between regular meals.

Gangway—The platform you walk on to get from the pier to the ship, and vice versa. Also, a command to clear the way, like, "Get out of my way." "Gangway" says it more clearly, quickly, and politely.

Godzilla—The name applies to the passenger who is programmed to complain about everything. Complaints about the cruise begin long before this passenger has left home. Although the complaints are often groundless, a really creative Godzilla can make them quite attention-grabbing. This type of passenger is not common—sometimes not even one per shipload, for which all are thankful. As we all know, the way to gain rewarding attention is through infecting fellow passengers with happiness and joy.

Handsomely—A command in line-handling meaning to do it quickly and in a seamanlike manner.

Hatchway—A doorway through a bulkhead, or the hole in the deck permitting access from one deck level to the next. Source of the expression, "Down the hatch."

Hawse pipes—The eyes, or openings, in the bow through which the anchor cable runs. Nautical saying, "Blow it out your hawse pipe."

Hawser—A rope too big to be a line. Generally used for towing.

Head—The bathroom, or toilet facility. So, if someone carrying tools knocks on your cabin door and says, "I want to work on your head," he's not a shrink but a plumber, shipboard variety.

The Distinctive Language of the Sea

Heave—Means to pull, push, or throw.

Heave to—To stop. With a vessel it means to stop with the bow pointed into the wind.

Helm—The tiller.

Hold—The space below the decks utilized for the stowage of ballast, cargo, and stores.

Hold water—Command to an oarsman to keep his oar still in the water.

Holystone—A large, flat stone, or fire brick, used to clean and whiten a vessel's wooden decks—so called because the seamen use it while on their knees.

House flag—Each shipping line has its own flag, which merchantmen fly for identification purposes.

Inboard—Toward the center of the vessel as opposed to outboard, or away from the center of the vessel.

Irish pennant—A line hanging over the side of a ship underway. Very unseamanlike. This term was probably dreamed up by the British Navy.

Jolly Roger—The pirate flag that you now see only in the movies. It is black with white skull and crossbones.

Jury rig—A substitute, temporary "fix" or repair while proper repairs are being made. Not the same as jury tamper.

Keel—The spine of the ship. It is the bottom midships member to which the ship's ribs are attached.

Knot—A manner of tying a line or joining two ropes together. There are many knots that have been developed for specialized uses. Also, a nautical mile, equal to 1.151 statute miles. Ship's travel is reckoned in knots, rather than miles per hour. Thus a knot is also a unit of speed. A ship traveling at 20 knots is doing 23 miles per hour.

Ladder—Exterior stairs on a ship. Face the direction of travel when using a ladder. Only a landlubber comes down facing the ladder. Ladders on cruise ships are generally built like stairways.

Landlubber—Someone unfamiliar with the sea and ships. Generally a term of derision, even among landlubbers.

Lazarette—A low head-room space below decks in the after part of a ship, used for provisions or spare parts.

Leeward (Pronounced loo'ard)—The opposite of windward. The side of the vessel away from the wind. Islands have windward and leeward sides, too.

Lifeboat—A small boat. Lifeboats are required by law. On cruise ships they are used for drills and also serve as shore launches when at anchor. Adherence to good seamanship and safety regulations minimizes the probability of actual use as a lifeboat.

Lifebuoy—That doughnut-shaped thing with the ship's name on it. Great prop for your cruise photos. If you should have occasion to use it to rescue someone who's fallen overboard, don't try to make a ringer, just try to throw it within reach. A direct hit could be fatal.

Line—A rope, when it is aboard ship, like the bowline, the stern line, the breastline. The only rope aboard ship is a coir rope. This is a very special rope that can be floated to a vessel in distress and then be used to tow her.

Log—The official book in which ship's position, weather, and all happenings aboard the vessel are recorded. Also, an instrument used to determine the speed of a vessel through the water.

Mizzenmast (Pronounced mizz'n m'st) Archaic—The sternmost mast on a square rigged sailing vessel. To sound salty, tell someone to "Go climb the mizz'n m'st."

Monkey paw or monkey fist—An intricate knot tied on the end of a heaving line. The heaving line is a light line thrown from ship to shore, during dock-

The Distinctive Language of the Sea

ing. Attached to the heaving line are the heavy lines used in securing the ship to the dock. The knot is so called because it looks like a monkey's fist. Usually a piece of lead is inserted into the fist. This practice is against rules and regulations because it is a safety hazard. But rules and regulations are of little help when throwing a heaving line into the wind.

Moor—To secure the ship as to a mooring buoy, or to drop anchor.

Officers—There are various ranks of officers and their insignia varies, too, according to the country of origin and customs of a particular ship line. Basically, the captain wears four gold stripes on his sleeve and wrinkles on his brow. The first officer wears three stripes, and looks very ambitious, for he is trying to attain that fourth stripe (and is usually qualified to do so). The second officer wears two stripes. The most harried, or most happy, is the youthful third officer with one stripe. The engineering officers have a similar ranking. The chief engineer is equivalent in rank to the first officer, and so on. In addition to the stripes, other insignias tell who is a deck officer, an engineering officer, or a medical officer.

Overhead—The ceiling above a deck.

Painter—Another rope—a light line used to secure a small boat.

Pier, or dock—The place in the harbor where the ship ties up.

Pilot—A skilled navigator who specializes in a specific port. He is picked up from the pilot boat as you enter his harbor. Because of his special knowledge of that harbor, he is charged with the responsibility of maneuvering your vessel in those waters.

Pitch—The action of the ship when the bow goes up and down while the stern goes down and up. Gives you a feeling of being at sea. Usually this motion is pleasant and does not cause *mal-de-mer*.

THE COMPLETE GUIDE TO A SUCCESSFUL CRUISE

Poop deck—Usually the furthermost aft top deck, reserved for the captain only. Most ships do not carry them anymore.

Port—Left-hand side of ship, as you look forward. Once called larboard but was too confusing with starboard. A designated area from which ships operate, like Port of Boston, Port of Los Angeles, and so on.

Porthole—That round window in the hull of the ship. It is best not to open it, unless you have permission.

Posh—Have you ever wondered about the origin of the word *posh* (meaning high quality or elegant service)? More than a century ago, the first steamships of the Peninsular and Oriental Steam Navigation Company (predecessor and parent company of today's P & O) began a steamer service from England to India. This was prior to the opening of the Suez Canal, and passengers traveled overland from the Mediterranean across the desert by camel to the Red Sea where they transferred to waiting steamers. As a courtesy, dignitaries were assigned the cooler cabins on the shady or *P*ort side of the ship going *O*ut to India, and the shady or *S*tarboard side coming *H*ome to England. Their tickets were accordingly stamped P.O.S.H.

Quarter—Not five nickels. It is the aft portion of the ship's side. There is port quarter and a starboard quarter.

Royal topgallant sail (Pronounced Royal T'gans'l)—Their days are gone, with the passing of the beautiful square rigged sailing vessels. The Royal T'gant was the very uppermost sail and used in light to moderate winds only.

Rudder—The thing on the stern that steers the ship. It is mounted with pintles and gudgeons, activated by the helmsman.

Rules of the road—Regulations enacted to provide safety of passage when two or more vessels are within sight or in near proximity.

The Distinctive Language of the Sea

Running light—There are two of these, one on each side of the ship. The port running light is red. The starboard running light is green. So, if you see another ship at night remember this:

"Green to Green, or Red to Red,
Perfect Safety, Go Ahead."

or the cadet version:

"Red to Red, or Green to Green,
For a Perfect Smash, Go Between."

Salt or old salt—Someone thoroughly familiar with ships, the sea, and its ways, and wants the world to know it. Not a landlubber. Don't ever call him one.

Schooner—A sailing vessel.

Screw—Also called the propeller. This is the device that transmits the power of the engine into the force that drives the ship through the water.

Scupper—A drain for removal of water collecting on exposed decks.

Scuttlebut—The container or cask of fresh water for drinking purposes once used by the crew. Since this was the place where the crew gathered, it was also the place to hear rumors. The casks are gone, but "scuttlebut" continues!

Sea dog—An old salt.

Seams—Where the ship's plates join together. They are usually welded together and are not readily observable.

Sextant—An instrument of navigation used to determine the angle of elevation of heavenly bodies—up in the sky, not on deck.

Shaft—The means of transmitting power from the engine(s) to the screw(s). Ofen called propeller shaft.

Shipshape—Neat, seamanlike.

Shot—A measurement of chain, usually 15 fathoms (90 feet).

Show a leg—An order to make haste.

Sick bay—The ship's hospital.
Skin—The inside or outside of a ship's plating. Not the kind exposed at the swimming pool.
Skipper—The captain, the "old man," and other appellations determined by the occasion. To his face, it is much better to address him as "captain."
Sky pilot—The chaplain.
Sounding—Determination of the depth of water beneath the keel, which is very important to know when in shallow water. On modern ships, this information is obtained from a depth sounder.
Splice the main brace—To have an alcoholic drink; in the old days it was rum.
Starboard—Right hand side of the ship when you are looking forward. If your cabin is odd-numbered, it is on the starboard side. If it is even numbered it is on the port side.
Stem—The part of the vessel rising up from the keel at the front, or bow. The stem is the most forward part of the bow.
Stern—The back end of the ship, usually blunt ended, or rounded.
Sun over the yardarm—When it is time for the first drink of the day.
Superstructure—The structure above the main deck.
Taffrail—The railing about the stern of the ship. Nice to lean on and have your pictures taken, or to watch the wake. Sometimes a taffrail log is mounted there for recording ship's speed.
Tar—An old term for a sailor, still used occasionally.
Tender—A small craft that services a ship. Can be operated by port personnel, or be carried aboard ship and operated by ship's personnel. Sometimes called a launch.
Thwart—What a funny name for something as simple as a seat in a small boat! Of course, the seat goes from one side to the other.
Tiller—A short piece of wood or iron which fits into the rudder head thus permitting the rudder to be turned.

The Distinctive Language of the Sea

Trick—The time spent by a crew member at a specific task during a watch, such as "His trick at the wheel."
Turn to—Begin to work.
Twice laid—Rope made up from old yarns.
Underway—When the ship is moving through the water, under power.
Unship—To take apart or to remove from its place.
Up behind—Another line-handling command meaning for all crew members to let go of a line at the same time.
Wake—The temporary track in the water left by a ship's passing.
Warp—To move a ship by use of line and winch rather than by use of engines or tugboats. This is generally done when adjusting the ship's position at a dock.
Watch—Usually, the four hour duty-cycle worked by the ship's crew.
Water breaker—A cask, or barricoe, carried in the lifeboat, containing fresh drinking water.
Weigh anchor—To raise the anchor.
Whistle—The ship's horn.
Windward—Towards the wind. The side of the vessel exposed to the wind.
Yaw—A motion of the ship when it departs from the course being steered, a sideways motion of the bow.

These are just a few nautical terms, but they're good for starters. The "Old Salt" will be pleased that you are trying, and your friends will be amazed at your acumen and knowledge of the sea. Try to use these terms in your cruise diary.

15

Displacement and Tonnage

The displacement of a vessel is the weight of water displaced by the ship floating freely. Archimedes discovered the principle that the weight of water displaced by a floating body is equal to the weight of that body. Thus, the displacement of a ship is equal to its weight. Ships' displacement varies according to the weight of the passengers and materials aboard. However, if you say a ship has a displacement of 30,000 tons, it refers to the ship's weight when fully loaded to its officially allowable capacity.

The tonnage of warships is simple; it refers to the displacement. With nonwarships, other tonnages become important.

a) *Light weight* is the weight of the vessel equipped fully with propelling machinery and equipment but without fuel or cargo.

b) *Dead weight* is the number of tons of stores of fuel and cargo a ship can carry officially. For the mathematical: it is equal numerically to the difference between the full load displacement and the light weight of the ship.

c) *Gross tonnage* = $\dfrac{\text{Vol. of ship below main deck in cu. ft.}}{100}$

d) *Net tonnage* = $\dfrac{\text{Vol. of cargo space in cu. ft.}}{100}$

So, you see, you have two measures of tonnage on a ship—actual weight and measures of cubic capacity as in gross tonnage and net tonnage.

The compass

As you know, the earth is an immense natural magnet with a pole in each hemisphere. The mariner's compass is a direction-indicating instrument consisting of either a simple magnet or a group of magnets fixed to a graduated circle pivoted at the center and allowed to swing freely in the horizontal plane. When unaffected by the ship's own magnetic fields, the compass, with its north seeking magnets, points towards the earth's magnetic north.

The earth's magnetic and geographic poles do not coincide and a magnetic compass points to the earth's magnetic north and not to true north.

The angular difference between true north and the direction in which the magnetic compass points when not influenced by the ship's magnetic properties is *variation*. The ship's magnetic properties influence the pointing of the magnetic compass and this is *deviation*. *Deviation* errors are known accurately for all points on the earth's surface. *Deviation* errors may be neutralized by "compensation." Compensation data for one

Displacement and Tonnage

approximate latitude is not necessarily correct for any other latitude.

The ship's own magnetic field is a resultant of construction. The direction in which the keel was laid, materials, and the amount of hammering are contributing factors.

Remember: Variation doesn't vary.
Deviation does.

Every ship carries a magnetic compass, but today's vessels navigate by use of the *gyro-compass*, which does point to true north at all times, not being affected by magnetism.

16

Classification Societies

The first classification society to be established was Lloyd's Register of Shipping, which dates from 1760, when its first function was marine insurance. Its activities as a classification organization did not begin until somewhat later. Other organizations, which are patterned largely after Lloyd's, are the American Bureau of Shipping, British Corporation Registry, Germanischer Lloyd's, and Registro Nazionale Italiano. Except for Great Britain, every maritime nation has one such organization which performs similar functions for the ships built in that nation. The functions are:

a) Publication of a register that contains the name, classifications, place and date of construction, present owner, tonnages, type of machinery and other pertinent information of all ships registered in that country.

b) Publication of ship construction instructions which are the shipbuilder's bible because they contain the rules by which dimensions of all structural members are determined.

c) Inspection of material is made by a society-employed inspector so that the ship may obtain proper classification.

d) Inspection of ships under construction is carried out to ascertain good workmanship and conformity to the rules.

e) Survey of ships is made. This function takes place during shipbuilding and periodically thereafter. It is done on request, often because the ship is up for sale or to grade the adequacy of repairs.

Crossing the International Date Line (180th Meridian)

The explanation for the change of dates when you cross the International Date Line can become quite involved and pedantic. It's easier to follow this simple rule:

When traveling westward, add one (1) to the date.

When traveling eastward, subtract one (1) from the date.

17

Turnaround

Voyage, travel, and change of place impart vigor
—Seneca

As your wonderful cruise draws to a close, you will feel all sorts of conflicting emotions. There will be the desire to return to familiar surroundings but at the same time you will wish that the cruise would last forever! You will have made new friends, experienced new adventures, and seen new sights. You will have been freed from tension and pressure.

Each time the ship turns around, we have a warm feeling during boarding because it seems as if half the passengers have sailed with us before on one ship or another.

Sometimes former passengers just come to watch the ship sail. You will find that your ship, during the cruise, has become more than an inanimate object. Each ship has its own charisma, and you can fall in love with more than one.

Every time I walk up the gangway, to board a new cruise ship, I never fail to be thrilled at the sight of her. I have lived on the oldest, smallest, newest, and biggest ships, and I truly love them all.

18

Disembarkation

FOR YOUR OWN COMFORT
AND
CONVENIENCE

* * * * *

AT DISEMBARKATION
YOU ARE ASKED NOT TO CROWD
THE GANGWAY BUT TO MAKE
YOURSELVES COMFORTABLE IN
THE PUBLIC ROOMS.
NO ONE IS ALLOWED ASHORE UN-
TIL ALL THE BAGGAGE IS OFF-
LOADED.
AN ANNOUNCEMENT WILL BE MADE
WHEN YOU MAY DISEMBARK.

The above notice probably will be published in the daily program on the last day of the cruise. I have given it a place of prominence in this book because I know that it is of such importance that it can make or break your cruise, so please read the following hints:

a) The last night at sea before reaching the port of disembarkation, place your luggage outside your cabin door.

THE COMPLETE GUIDE TO A SUCCESSFUL CRUISE

b) You may keep a small piece of hand luggage with you for your nightwear, shaving kit, make-up kit, etc.

(c) The only clothing to keep with you is the clothing you will wear at disembarkation.

19

Immigration

The immigration authorities usually water-taxi out to the ship and board so that passengers can go through their line before the ship docks. Immigration is solely for the purpose of determining your citizenship—*it has nothing to do with customs.*

Every member of each family must go personally through the line. No one can go for the rest of the family. If your ship is to arrive early in the morning in home port, no one should stay in bed and expect the other passengers to wait for them, because *not one* piece of luggage is allowed to be removed from the ship until every last passenger has been processed through the immigration line.

You may have enjoyed a fabulous farewell party the night before, but you must force yourself to get up and go through the line (it goes very fast). Then you can go to breakfast and/or go back to bed and take a snooze until you hear the announcement on the loudspeaker that passengers are allowed to disembark.

Some passengers dash to the gangway so that they can be among the first off the ship. They are in for a long, tiring wait.

The smart passengers either make themselves comfortable in their cabins or in the public rooms. Some play cards or read, but most are busy exchanging addresses and saying farewell to new-found friends.

When you go through the immigration line, *although it has nothing to do with customs*, bring your Customs Declaration and identification papers.

Some ships perform immigration procedures on the dock upon your arrival. On all ships your Customs Declaration will be slipped under your cabin door the last day at sea. Please complete it (one per family) and hand it to the officials supervising the immigration line. They will use it to check your name on their immigration list along with other identification. Your Customs Declaration will be handed back to you so that you may have it for the Customs line as you pick up your luggage on the dock later.

20

Cruising Pictorialized: The Dream Merchants

*Whenever I find myself growing grim
about the mouth; whenever it is a damp,
drizzly November in my soul; and especially
whenever it requires a strong moral principle
to prevent me from methodically knocking people's hats
off—then, I account it high time to get to sea. There is
nothing surprising in this. If they but knew it,
almost all men in their degree cherish very nearly the
same feelings towards the ocean with me.*
—Herman Melville, *Moby Dick*

The pictures in this book are only a smidgen of the photos I wish we had space for, but I hope they will suffice to help you decide that you will spend your next vacation on the sea.

I want to mention that even though these ships may sail from ports far from your home, there are air/sea packages on many lines. Your travel agent can arrange air/sea package cruises on any of the following airlines:

British Airways
Lufthansa German Airlines
KLM Royal Dutch Airlines

Western Airlines Continental Airlines
National Airlines American Airlines
Delta Airlines Pan American Airlines
Air New Zealand Trans World Airlines
Philippine Airlines United Airlines

Many other airlines offer these air/sea packages. They will save you money as well as time. In fact, the fly/cruise combination has shaken the travel industry like a sonic boom. Because cruise lines absorb much of the air-fare (in some cases all of it), fly/cruise programs are a new vacation value. Some lines also offer cruise/stay programs for those who wish to prolong their holiday in one particular port. Your travel agent can arrange this for you.

I have purposely omitted the addresses of the various cruise lines because they prefer you to book through your travel agent, at no extra cost to you.

Cruising can be just as expensive or inexpensive as you wish. Here you will find sailings ranging from three-day quickie-voyages to leisurely round-the-world journeys. Whether you join the ship near a home port or take advantage of an air/sea program, the choices available are staggering.

Cruising Pictorialized

Carras Cruises. M.T.S. *Daphne* and M.T.S. *Danae,* luxurious sister ships, carry passengers to ports of call in the Caribbean, Mexico, and the Mediterranean. The crew puts on beautiful folklore shows.

THE COMPLETE GUIDE TO A SUCCESSFUL CRUISE

Chandris Lines/Chandris Cruises. Meet the liners that will take you cruising in the Mediterranean, Black Sea, Atlantic Isles, and also to the land of the midnight sun, Alaska. Whether they carry over 1,000 passengers like the giant *Britanis* (pictured), or 350 passengers like the lovely *Fiorita*, they are all operated to give you the time of your life.

Cruising Pictorialized

Commodore Cruise Line, Ltd. Shown here is the M.S. *Boheme* as it leaves the Port of Miami on one of its weekly four-islands cruises. Its ports will be Puerto Plata, St. Thomas, San Juan, and Cap Haitien. This line also has the beautiful M.S. *Caribe* which cruises to Montego Bay, Port Antonio, Port-au-Prince, and Puerto Plata. Both these ships have single cabins with connecting doubles, as well as regular cabins.

THE COMPLETE GUIDE TO A SUCCESSFUL CRUISE

Costa Line, Inc. This large fleet, which includes the M.S. *Federico "C"* (pictured), offers every kind of cruise, from three days to around the world.

Cruising Pictorialized

Cruise East. Cruise East, Los Angeles, sails the M.S. *Rasa Sayang* on 14-day cruises. Passengers may embark and disembark at any of the six ports of call from Singapore to Indonesia and Malaysia.

Cunard Line Ltd. The *Queen Elizabeth II* is Cunard's transatlantic liner crossing between New York and Southampton.
She also makes Caribbean and world cruises. The *Countess* (pictured), based in San Juan, sails a seven-day Caribbean route. Her sister ship, the *Princess*, sails out of Fort Lauderdale.

Cruising Pictorialized

Delta Queen Steamboat Co. With their flags a-flyin' and calliopes blowin', the *Mississippi Queen* (left), a new luxurious stern wheeler, and the *Delta Queen* (below), the last of the old-time steamboats, sail on cruises lasting from 2 to 19 nights. Embarkation points are New Orleans, St. Louis, St. Paul, Pittsburgh, Nashville, and their home port of Cincinnati.

Eastern Steamship Lines Inc. The magnificent S.S. *Emerald Seas* sails on three- and four-night cruises to Nassau and Freeport from the Port of Miami. One of the ship's many features is an all-night gambling casino!

Cruising Pictorialized

Epirotiki Lines, Inc. The ships in this line offer cosmopolitan ambience, international cuisine, and personalized service. You can spend many days, or just one or two, on the historic Greek islands of Delos, Mykonos, Hydra, Santorini—to name just a few. This company also has worldwide cruising. Pictured is the M.T.S. *Jason.*

Flagship Cruises. M.S. *Kungsholm* is a world of comfort and luxury afloat—an ideal ship for warm hospitality, impeccable service, and glamorous surroundings. It features Scandanavian officers, English-speaking cruise staff, Italian dining room stewards, and international and American cuisine.

Cruising Pictorialized

German Rhine Line–Rhine Cruise Agency. Cruises on the Rhine offer you a spectacular view of the treasures to be found in the heart of Europe. You'll see sparkling cities, famous cathedrals, lush vineyards, ancient castles, fortresses, and robbers' lairs while enjoying the amenities of a deluxe hotel. Here is one of eight modern liners that offer a choice of nearly 400 different sailing dates.

THE COMPLETE GUIDE TO A SUCCESSFUL CRUISE

Hellenic Mediterranean Lines Co., Ltd. The M.S. *Aquarius* (pictured) and M.S. *Castalia* offer seven-day cruises that visit six strikingly beautiful Greek islands and then go northward across the Aegean to Ephesus and Istanbul.

Cruising Pictorialized

Holland American Cruises. The S.S. *Statendam* (left) sails to Bermuda and the Caribbean. The S.S. *Rotterdam* (below) makes Nassau, Bermuda, and around-the-world cruises. In the spring, the M.S. *Prinsendam* makes an interesting "positioning" voyage from Singapore (including Shanghai as one of the ports) to Vancouver, Canada. It goes the other direction in the autumn. Monarch Cruise Lines Inc., a division of Holland American Line, has the *Monarch Star* and *Monarch Sun* featuring trips to Alaska via Panama Canal, Caribbean, and South American cruises. Westours in Seattle charters the *Monarch Star* and the M.S. *Prinsendam* for the Alaskan season.

THE COMPLETE GUIDE TO A SUCCESSFUL CRUISE

Home Lines Inc. The S.S. *Oceanic* and the S.S. *Doric*'s Italian personnel render service that recalls the elegance of a bygone era. Here the *Doric* is docked in Bermuda. There are also sailings to Nassau and the Caribbean with the same fine Italian hands.

Cruising Pictorialized

Lauro Line Cruises, Inc.
The M.S. *Achille Lauro* and the M.S. *Angelina Lauro* (shown) are 24,000 tons each. They are of Italian registry with Italian crews, offering cruises to Genoa, Naples, Alexandria, Port Said, Beirut, Haifa, Istanbul, and Piraeus-Athens. The M.S. *Achille Lauro* makes an around-the-world cruise in 90 days. You may embark in Genoa, San Francisco, or Los Angeles.

THE COMPLETE GUIDE TO A SUCCESSFUL CRUISE

March Shipping Corporation. The M.V. *Odessa*, M.S. *Kazakhstan* (shown), and the M.S. *Alexander Pushkin* operate from St. Lawrence River points and also have transatlantic sailings. Among the highlights of cruises on these Russian ships are the colorful folkloric dances and Balalaika shows presented by the crews.

Cruising Pictorialized

Negros Navigation Co. See the Philippines —7,100 beautiful islands—by sea. You may choose from three routes, Fiesta Islands, Sun Islands, or the Emerald Isles cruises.

THE COMPLETE GUIDE TO A SUCCESSFUL CRUISE

Norwegian Caribbean Lines.
For a carefree vacation sail
on one of the four sparkling
Norwegian-registered vessels:
M.S. *Skyward*, M.S. *Starward*
(shown), M.S. *Southward*,
and M.S. *Sunward II*.
Seven-day cruises to the Caribbean
and three- and four-night cruises
to Nassau and the Out Islands
are offered.

Cruising Pictorialized

Paquet French Cruises. This French line has cruises to Alaska, the Caribbean, South America, the Greek Islands, and Europe. The ships offer "Gourmet Cruises," and for music lovers, the renowned "Music Festivals at Sea" aboard the M.S. *Renaissance*, pictured here.

The Peninsular and Oriental Steam Navigation Co. (registered in Britain). This company's well known *Arcadia, Canberra* (left), and *Oriana* cover more than half the globe. You can thrill to foreign lands, fascinating people, a variety of languages, whether you've a specific destination or just want to sail away into the sunset. Both full and partial cruises are available. Also shown is the line's *Pacific Princess* (below) of Princess Cruises.

Photograph courtesy of Princess Cruises, Los Angeles

Cruising Pictorialized

Prince of Fundy Cruises. These exciting one-day cruises include a two-hour stopover in Nova Scotia, Canada. The new M.S. *Caribe* leaves Portland, Maine, every evening and arrives in Yarmouth the following morning. After a two-hour stopover, the ship returns to Portland. Packaged cruise/car stopovers are available for longer vacations (yes, they take your car along, too).

THE COMPLETE GUIDE TO A SUCCESSFUL CRUISE

Prudential Cruises. Join anywhere, leave anywhere, or combine sea, air, and land travel to some of the most exotic places in the world. These cruise liners carry cargo plus 100 passengers. This is the only American shipping company that still offers passenger service. Activities are not as extensive as those on a regular cruise ship, but there are swimming pools, deck sports, movies, and special dinners highlighting the cuisine of the South American destinations. Pictured here is the *Santa Mariana*.

Royal Caribbean Cruise Line, Inc.
A once-in-a-lifetime shot of the
Royal Caribbean fleet in St. Thomas.
Left to right are the *Sun Viking*,
the *Nordic Prince*, and
the *Song of Norway*.

Royal Cruise Lines. The M.S. *Golden Odyssey* (shown here in the Panama Canal Locks) offers cruises from Los Angeles to Athens. Royal Cruise Lines also sail to Mexico, the Mediterranean, and Russia. The crews are Greek.

Cruising Pictorialized

Royal Viking Line. This line's three ships cruise all over the world. Pictured here are the scenic transit of the Panama Canal (right) and the beautiful *Royal Viking Star* at night (below).

THE COMPLETE GUIDE TO A SUCCESSFUL CRUISE

Sitmar Cruises. The T.S.S. *Fairsea* and the T.S.S. *Fairwind,* twin ships of 25,000 tons, provide you with every shipboard amenity. Both ships are pictured here in Acapulco Bay. They also cruise to the Caribbean, South America, Canada, and Alaska.

Cruising Pictorialized

Sun Line (Greek registry). These ships go to places everybody has heard of—St. Thomas, the Yucatan, Jamaica—and to places unknown to all but the seasoned traveler—Iles des Saintes, Bequia, and a trip up South America's Orinoco River to an outpost on the edge of civilization. The 18,000-ton flag ship, the *Stella Solaris* (above), the 6,000-ton *Stella Oceanis* (below), and the 4,000-ton *Stella Maris* cruise the Aegean and Mediterranean every summer and the Caribbean and South America in the winter. With élan, the officers and crew perform Greek dances for you and will teach you to dance the Syrtski.

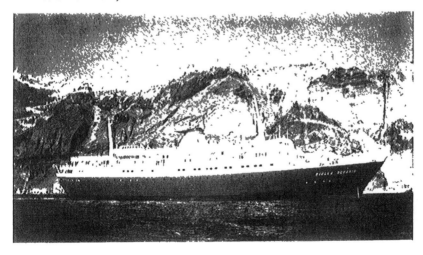

THE COMPLETE GUIDE TO A SUCCESSFUL CRUISE

Windjammer "Barefoot" Cruises. Organized in 1947 by Captain Mike Burke to keep alive the tradition of the great sailing ships, these unique "barefoot" vacations are tempered with modern comfort. "Shipmates" need not be sailors, nor even lend a hand; all they need is a love of the outdoors and a spirit of adventure. This is the largest fleet of sailing ships afloat.

21

Customs Hints For Returning U.S. Residents

This chapter is devoted to United States Customs regulations and procedures for U.S. residents going abroad. Your knowledge and use of this information will enable inspectors, upon your return, to complete your baggage examination without difficulty.

I want to impress upon you, first of all, the importance of attending the *Cruise Director's Disembarkation Talk*, which will be held the last day out, for you will learn much at this lecture.

Each ship has its own routine for organizing disembarkation. But all ships try to make sure that you have a way of tagging your luggage so that you will find the various pieces near each other on the dock.

Please remember that the cruise line has no control over our customs regulations or their mode of operation. It may go fast—or it may be slow. Plan on the latter, so you—and waiting friends—won't be disappointed. Allow for one or two hours delay after docking.

For example: Your ship returns to home port at 8:00 A.M., but no one will be allowed off the ship until *all* luggage has been taken ashore. So you probably won't *start* disembarking until 9 A.M. Then you must find your luggage and go through customs. So it may be 9:30 or 10 A.M. before you can leave the docks.

Please *don't* make plane reservations too close to your ship's arrival time.

Allow at least four hours between your ship's docking time and your plane's departure. Then you'll be ready to go through disembarkation procedures in a relaxed state of mind. Instead of clenching your teeth and frowning and looking at your watch every other second, you'll be attending to something much more important—making plans to see your wonderful new friends again!

Delay in customs clearance may be caused by large groups of ship passengers arriving at the same time or by an unusually close inspection to prevent the smuggling of dangerous drugs and other contraband. In this endeavor, the understanding and cooperation of the traveler are necessary. To make your homecoming as pleasant as your leaving, take a few minutes and become familiar with these customs hints.

Your declaration

All articles acquired abroad and in your possession at the time of your return must be declared. This includes:

a. Gifts presented to you while abroad, such as wedding or birthday presents.

b. Repairs or alterations made to any articles taken abroad and returned, whether or not repairs or alterations were free of charge.

c. Items you have been requested to bring home for another person.

d. Any articles you intend to sell or use in your business.

The price actually paid for each article must be stated on your declaration in U.S. currency, or its equivalent, in country of acquisition. If the article was not purchased, obtain its fair retail value in the country in which it was acquired.

Note: The wearing or use of any article acquired abroad does not exempt it from duty. It must be declared at the price you paid for it. The customs officer will make an appropriate reduction in its value for wear and use.

Oral declaration

Custom declaration forms are distributed on cruise ships and should be prepared in advance of arrival for presentation to the immigration and customs inspectors. Fill out the identification portion of the declaration form. You may declare orally to the customs inspector the articles you acquired abroad, if you have not exceeded the duty-free exemption allowed. A customs officer may, however, ask you to prepare a written list if he thinks it is necessary.

Written declaration

A written declaration will be necessary when:

a. The total fair retail value of articles acquired abroad exceeds $100.

b. More than one quart of alcoholic beverages or more than 100 cigars are included.

c. Some of the items are not intended for your personal or household use, such as commercial samples, items for sale or use in your business, or articles you are bringing home for another person.

d. A customs duty or internal revenue tax is collectible on any article in your possession.

Family declaration

The head of a family may make a joint declaration for all members residing in the same household and returning with him to the United States. Example: A family of four may bring in articles free of duty valued up to $400 retail value on one declaration, even if the articles acquired by one member of the family exceeds his $100 exemption.

Your exemptions

In clearing United States Customs, a traveler is considered either a "returning resident of the United States" or a "nonresident."

Generally speaking, if you leave the United States for purposes of traveling, working, or studying abroad and return to resume residency in the United States, you are considered a returning resident by customs.

Articles acquired aboard and brought into the United States are subject to applicable duty and internal revenue tax, but as a returning resident, you are allowed certain exemptions from paying duty on items obtained while abroad.

$100 exemption

Articles totaling $100 (based on the fair retail value of each item in the country where obtained) may be entered free of duty, subject to the limitations on liquors and cigars, if:

    a. Articles were acquired as an incident of your trip for your personal or household use.

    b. You bring the articles with you at the time of your return to the United States and they are properly declared to customs. Articles purchased and left for

Customs Hints

alterations or other reasons cannot be applied to your $100 exemption when shipped to follow at a later date.

    c. You are returning from a stay abroad of at least 48 hours. Example:

A resident who leaves United States territory at 1:30 P.M. on June 1 would complete the required 48-hour period at 1:30 P.M. on June 3. This time limitation does not apply if you are returning from Mexico or the Virgin Islands of the United States.

    d. You have not used this $100 exemption, or any part of it, within the preceding 30-day period. Also, your exemption is not cumulative. If you use a portion of your exemption on entering the United States, then you must wait for 30 days before you are entitled to another exemption other than a $10 exemption.

Cigars and cigarettes

Not more than 100 cigars may be included in your exemption. Products of Cuban tobacco are prohibited. There is no limitation on the number of cigarettes that may be imported for your personal use. This exemption is available to each person regardless of age. Your cigarettes, however, may be subject to a tax imposed by state and local authorities.

Liquor

One quart (32 fluid ounces) of alcoholic beverages may be included in this exemption, if you are 21 years of age or older. Alcoholic beverages in excess of the one quart limitation are subject to duty and internal revenue tax. (Note: In California, only one quart of alcoholic beverage is allowable.)

The importation must be for your own use or for a gift and not in violation of the laws of the state in which you arrive. *State laws vary*. Information about state restrictions and taxes can be obtained from the Department of Revenue of the state in question.

United States postal laws prohibit the shipment of alcoholic beverages by mail.

Know your home port's state liquor laws!

$200 exemption

If you return directly or indirectly from the Virgin Islands of the United States, American Samoa, or Guam, you may receive a customs exemption of $200 (based on the fair retail value of the articles in the country where acquired). Not more than $100 of this exemption may be applied to merchandise obtained elsewhere than in these islands.

Residents 21 years of age or older may enter one U.S. gallon of alcoholic beverages (128 fluid ounces) free of duty and tax, provided not more than one quart of this amount is acquired elsewhere than in these islands.

Other provisions under the $100 exemption apply.

$10 exemption

If you cannot claim the $100 or $200 exemption because of the 30-day or 48-hour minimum limitations, you may bring in, free of duty and tax, articles acquired abroad for your personal or household use if the total fair retail value does not exceed $10. This is an individual exemption and may not be grouped with other members of a family on one customs declaration.

You may include any of the following: 50 cigarettes, 10 cigars, 4 ounces of alcoholic beverages, or 4 ounces of alcoholic perfume.

If any article brought with you is subject to duty or tax, or if the total value of all dutiable articles exceeds $10, no article may be exempted from duty or tax.

Infants and children returning to the United States are entitled to the same exemption as adults (except for alcoholic beverages). Children born abroad, who have

Customs Hints

never resided in the United States, are not eligible for this exemption but are eligible for exemptions as nonresidents.

Over your exemption?

Articles imported in excess of your customs exemption will be subject to duty calculated by the customs inspector, unless the items are entitled to free entry or prohibited.

The inspector will place the items having the highest rate of duty under your exemption and any duty due will be assessed upon the lower rated items. Except for custom-made articles, duty assessed will be based on the wholesale value of the articles as determined by the examining officer.

Payment of duty, required at the time of your arrival, may be made by any of the following ways:

    a. U.S. currency (foreign currency is not acceptable).

    b. Personal check in the exact amount of duty, drawn on a national or state bank or trust company of the United States, made payable to the "U.S. Customs Service."

    c. Government check, money orders or traveler's checks are acceptable if they do not exceed the amount of the duty by more than $50. (Second endorsements are not acceptable. Identification must be presented; e.g. traveler's passport or Social Security card.)

Gifts (bona fide) of not more than $10 ($20 if shipped from U.S. Virgin Islands, American Samoa, or Guam) in fair retail value where shipped, can be received by friends and relations in the United States free of duty or tax, if the same person does not receive more than $10 in gift shipments in one day. The "day" in reference is the day in which the parcel(s) is received for customs processing.

If any article imported is subject to duty and tax, or if the total value of all articles exceeds $10, no article may be exempt from duty or tax.

Write "Unsolicited Gift—Value Under $10" in large letters on the outside of the package. Alcoholic beverages and tobacco products are not included in this privilege, nor are alcoholic perfumes valued at more than $1.

Gifts mailed to friends and relatives are not declared by you on your return to the States. A "gift" parcel sent by a traveler to himself or anyone traveling with him will be subject to applicable duty and tax.

Gifts accompanying you are considered to be for your personal use and may be included within your exemption. This includes gifts given to you by others while abroad and those you intend to give to others after your return. Gifts intended for business or promotional purposes may not be included.

Personal belongings of United States origin are entitled to entry free of duty. Personal belongings taken abroad, such as worn clothing, etc., may be sent home by mail before you return and receive free entry provided they have not been altered or repaired while abroad. These packages should be marked "American Goods Returned." When a claim of United States origin is made, marking on the article to so indicate facilitates customs processing.

Some products from certain developing countries may enter the United States free of duty under the Generalized System of Preferences (GSP). This will be discussed at length at the end of the chapter.

Prohibited and restricted articles

Because customs inspectors are stationed at ports of entry and along our land and sea borders, they are often called upon to enforce laws and requirements of other government agencies. For example, the Department of Agriculture is responsible for preventing the entry of injurious pest, plant, and animal diseases into the United States. The customs officer cannot ignore the agriculture requirements—the risk of costly damage to our crops, poultry, and livestock industry is too great.

Certain articles considered injurious or detrimental to the general welfare of the United States are prohibited entry by law. Among these are absinthe, lottery tickets, narcotics and dangerous drugs, obscene articles and publications, seditious and treasonable materials, hazardous articles (e.g. fireworks, dangerous toys, toxic or poisonous substances), and switchblade knives.

Other items must meet special requirements before they can be released. You will be given a receipt for any articles retained by customs.

Biological materials
Biological materials of public health or veterinary importance (disease organisms and vectors for research and educational purposes) require import permits. Write to the Foreign Quarantine Program, U.S. Public Health Service, Center for Disease Control, Atlanta, Ga. 30333.

Books
Books protected by U.S. copyright cannot be brought into the United States if they are unauthorized foreign reprints. Books bearing a notice falsely claiming copyright in the United States are similarly prohibited. Also, some books by U.S. authors or books first published in the United States may not be imported into the United States in foreign editions unless they accompany the traveler and are for his personal use.

Cultural property

Cultural property, such as pre-Columbian monumental and architectural sculpture or murals, may need an export certificate from certain Latin American countries in order to be imported.

Firearms and ammunition

Firearms and ammunition are subject to restrictions and import permits approved by the Bureau of Alcohol, Tobacco, and Firearms (ATF). Applications to import may be made only by or through a licensed importer, dealer, or manufacturer. Weapons, ammunition, or other devices prohibited by the National Firearms Act will not be admitted into the United States, unless by specific authorization of ATF.

No import permit is required when it is proven that the firearms or ammunition were previously taken out of the United States by the person who is returning with such firearms or ammunition. To facilitate reentry, persons may have them registered before departing from the United States at any U. S. customs office or ATF field office. However, not more than three nonautomatic firearms and 1,000 cartridges will be registered for any one person. Quantities in excess of those indicated are subject to the export licensing requirements of the Office of Munitions Control, Department of State, Washington, D.C., 20520.

For further information, contact the Bureau of Alcohol, Tobacco and Firearms, Department of the Treasury, Washington, D.C. 20226.

Residents of the United States carrying firearms or ammunition with them to other countries should consult in advance the customs officials or the respective embassies of those countries as to their regulations.

Fruits, vegetables, plants

Cuttings, seeds, and unprocessed plant products are

Customs Hints

either prohibited from entering the country or require an import permit. Every single plant, plant product, fruit or vegetable must be declared to the customs officer and must be presented for inspection, no matter how free of pests it appears to be.

Canned or processed items are admissible, as well as bakery products.

Applications for import permits or requests for information should be addressed to Quarantines, Department of Agriculture, Federal Center Bldg., Hyattsville, Md. 20782.

Gold

All gold, including gold coins, medals, and bullion formerly prohibited, may be brought into the United States.

Meats, livestock, poultry

Meats, livestock, poultry, and their by-products are either prohibited or restricted from entering the United States, depending on animal disease condition in country of origin. This includes fresh, frozen, dried, cured, cooked, or canned items. You should contact the Animal and Plant Health Inspection Service, USDA, Hyattsville, Maryland 20782, for detailed requirements.

All prohibited importations will be seized and destroyed unless the importer returns them immediately to their country of origin.

Merchandise

Copies of Foreign Assets Control Regulations, Cuban Assets Control Regulations and Rhodesian Sanction Regulations may be obtained from the Office of Foreign Assets Control, Department of the Treasury, Washington, D. C. 20220.

Articles of Chinese origin, formerly prohibited, may

now be brought or shipped into the United States. If any items are subject to duty, the rate will be considerably higher than the rate applied to goods imported from non-Communist countries.

Money
Money (coin or currency), travelers checks, money orders, and negotiable instruments in bearer form to which title passes with delivery, may be brought into or taken out of the United States. Persons importing or exporting an amount of more than $5,000, however, are required to file a report of the transaction with U. S. Customs. Ask a customs officer for a form at the time you arrive or depart with such amounts.

Narcotics and dangerous drugs
Narcotics and dangerous drugs are prohibited entry by law; therefore a traveler requiring *medicines* containing habit-forming drugs or narcotics (i.e., cough medicines, diuretics, heart drugs, tranquilizers, sleeping pills, depressants, stimulants, etc.) should have all drugs, medicinals, and similar products properly identified. He should carry only such quantity as might normally be carried by an individual having some sort of health problem and, in addition, should have either a prescription or written statement from his personal physician that the medicinals are being used under a doctor's direction and are necessary for the traveler's physical well-being while traveling.

Customs pointers
Keep your sales slips. Your sales slips will be helpful in making out your declaration.
Packing your baggage. Pack your baggage in a manner that will make inspection easy. *Do your best to pack separately the articles you have acquired abroad.* When

the customs officer asks you to open your luggage, do so without hesitation.

Photographic film. All imported photographic films, which accompany a traveler, if not for commercial purpose, may be released without examination by customs unless there is reason to believe they contain objectional matter.

Films prohibited entry are those that contain obscene matter, advocate treason or insurrection against the United States, advocate forcible resistance to any law of the United States, or those that threaten the life of or infliction of bodily harm upon any person in the United States.

Developed or undeveloped U.S. film exposed abroad (except motion-picture film to be used for commercial purposes) may enter free of duty and need not be included in your customs exemption.

Foreign film purchased abroad and prints made abroad are dutiable but may be included in your customs exemption.

Film manufactured in the United States and exposed abroad may be mailed home. Use the mailing device or prepaid mailer provided by the manufacturer or processing laboratory for this purpose. Mark the outside wrapper "Undeveloped photographic film of U.S. manufacture—Examine with care."

Delivery can be expedited if the package is addressed to your dealer or a processing laboratory for finishing. If package is a prepaid processing mailer, no customs arrangements need be made. If not, arrange before you leave for the laboratory or dealer to accept and enter the film. If delivery is refused, the film must be sent back to a warehouse and becomes subject to a storage fee.

Delivery can be expedited if the package is addressed to the manufacturer of the film. All customs requirements will be taken care of by the manufacturer who is well-informed on customs procedures.

If none of the above suggestions can be used, address the package to yourself.

Shipping hints

Merchandise acquired abroad may be sent home by you or by the store where purchased. As these items do not accompany you on your return, they cannot be included in your customs exemptions, and are subject to duty when received in the United States. Duty cannot be prepaid.

All incoming shipments must be cleared through U.S. Customs. Customs employees cannot, by law, perform entry tasks for the importing public, but they will advise and give information to importers about customs requirements.

Customs collects no fee except the customs duty (if any) as provided for in the tariff schedules. Any other charges paid on import shipments are for handling by freight forwarders, commercial brokers, or for other delivery services.

Note: Customhouse brokers are not U.S. Customs employees. Fees charged by the brokers are based on the amount of work done, not on the value of the suitcase of personal effects or of the tourist purchase you shipped. The fee may seem excessive to you in relation to the value of the shipment. The National Customs Brokers & Forwarders Association is well aware of the difficulties and excessive expense incurred by tourists shipping items home. Their advice is "Ship the easy way—take it with you in your baggage or send it by parcel post prepaid."

Mail shipments (including parcel post) have proven to be more convenient and less costly for travelers.

Customs Hints

Parcels must meet the mail requirements of the exporting country as to weight, size, and measurement.

The U.S. Postal Service sends all incoming foreign mail shipments to customs for examination. Packages free of customs duty are returned to the Postal Service for delivery to you by your home post office without additional postage, handling costs, or other fees.

For packages containing dutiable articles, the customs officer will attach a mail entry showing the amount of duty to be paid and return the parcel to the U.S. Postal Service. Your postman will collect the duty and a postal handling fee when he delivers the package. If for any reason duty is later refunded, the postal handling fee will also be refunded. If an adjustment is made with a partial refund of duty, postal handling fee will not be refunded.

Express shipments may be sent to the United States from Canada and Mexico and by air freight from other countries. The express company or its representative, when properly licensed, usually acts as the customhouse broker for you and clears the merchandise through customs. A fee is charged for this service.

Freight shipments, whether or not they are free of duty at the time of importation, must clear customs at the first port of arrival into the United States, *or* if you choose, the merchandise may be forwarded in customs custody (in bond) from the port of arrival to another customs port of entry for customs clearance.

All arrangements for customs clearance and forwarding in bond must be made by you or someone you designate to act for you. Frequently, a freight forwarder in a foreign country will handle all the necessary arrangements, including the clearance through customs in the United States by a customhouse broker. A fee is charged for this service. This fee is not a Customs charge. If a foreign seller consigns a shipment to a broker or agent in the United States, the freight charge is usually paid only to the first port of arrival in the United States. This means there will be additional inland transportation or freight forwarding charges, brokers' fees, insurance, and other items.

An individual may also effect the customs clearance of a single noncommercial shipment for you if it is not possible for you to personally secure the release of the goods. You must authorize and empower the individual in writing to execute the customs declaration and the entry for you as your unpaid agent. The written authority provided to the individual should be addressed to the "Officer in Charge of Customs" at the port of entry.

Storage charges. Freight and express packages delivered before you return (without prior arrangements for acceptance) will be placed in storage by customs after 5 days, at the expense and risk of the owner. If not claimed within one year, the items will be sold.

Mail parcels not claimed within 30 days will be returned to the sender.

Rates of duty

This abbreviated list of the most popular items imported by tourists, with rates of duty, is intended to be used as an advisory guide only. The customs officer examining your baggage will determine the rates of duty if you have dutiable articles. (Notes: Rates of duty on goods produced in Communist countries are considerably higher. Consult a customs office about these rates.)

Customs Hints

Alcoholic beverages

	Int. Rev. Tax	Customs duty
Beer	$9 bbl. (31 gal.)	6¢ per gal.
Brandy	$10.50*	50¢* to $5*
Gin	$10.50*	50¢*
Liqueurs	$10.50*	50¢*
Rum	$10.50*	$1.75*
Whisky*		
Scotch	$10.50*	51¢
Irish	$10.50*	51¢
Other	$10.50*	62¢
Wine		
Sparkling	$2.40 to $3.40	$1.17
Still	17¢ to $2.25	31 1/2¢ to $1

Antiques produced prior to 100 years before the date of entry—Free. (Have proof of antiquity obtained from seller.)

Automobiles, passenger—3%

Bags, hand, leather—8½ to 10%

Bamboo, manufactures of—12½%

Beads
  Imitation precious and semi-precious stones—7 to 13%
  Ivory—10%

Binoculars
  Prism—20%
  Opera and field glasses—8½%

Books
  Foreign author or foreign language—Free

Cameras
  Motion picture, over $50 each—6%
  Still, over $10 each—7½%

---

*Per U.S. gallon (128 fluid ounces) if under 100 proof. Duty and tax are based on proof gallon if 100 proof or over.

Cases, leather—8½ to 10%
Lenses—12½%

Candy
Sweetened chocolate bars—5%
Other—7%

Chess Sets—10%

China
Bone—17½%
Nonbone, other than tableware—22½%

China tableware, nonbone, available in 77-piece sets
Valued not over $10 per set—10¢ doz. + 48%
Valued over $10 but not over $24 per set—10¢ doz. + 55%
Valued over $24 but not over $56 per set—10¢ doz. + 36%
Valued over $56 per set—5¢ doz. + 18%

Cigarette Lighters
Pocket, valued at over 42¢ each—22½%
Table—12%

Clocks
Valued over $5 but not over $10 each—75¢ + 16% + 6¼¢ for each jewel
Valued over $10 each—$1.12 ea. + 16% + 6¼¢ for each jewel

Cork, manufactures of—18%

Dolls and parts—17½%

Drawings (works of art)
Original—Free
Copies, done entirely by hand—Free

Earthenware tableware, available in 77-piece sets
Valued not over $3.30 per set—5¢ doz. + 14%
Valued over $3.30 but not over $22 per set—10¢ doz. + 21%
Valued over $22 per set—5¢ doz. + 10½%

Figurines, china—12½% to 22½%

Film, imported, not qualifying for free entry is dutiable as follows:

Customs Hints

Exposed motion-picture film in any form on which pictures or sound and pictures have been recorded, developed or not developed, is dutiable at 48/100ths of a cent per linear foot.

Other exposed or exposed and developed film would be classifiable as photographs, dutiable at 4% of their value.

Flowers, artificial, plastic—21%

Fruit, prepared—35% or under

Fur
   Wearing apparel—8½ to 18½%
   Other manufactures of—8½ to 18½%

Furniture
   Wood, chairs—8½%
   Wood, other than chairs—5%

Glass tableware valued not over $1 each— 20 to 50%

Gloves
   Not lace or net, plain vegetable fibers, woven—25%
   Wool, over $4 per dozen—37½¢ lb. + 18½%
   Fur—10%
   Horsehide or cowhide—15%

Golf Balls—6%

Handkerchiefs
   Cotton, hand embroidered—4¢ ea. + 40%
   Cotton, plain—25%
   Other vegetable fiber, plain—9%

Iron, travel type, electric—5½%

Ivory, manufactures of—6%

Jade
   Cut, but not set and suitable for use in the manufacture of jewelry—2½%
   Other articles of jade—21%

Jewelry, precious metal or stone
   Silver chief value, valued not over $18 per dozen—27½%
   Other—12%

THE COMPLETE GUIDE TO A SUCCESSFUL CRUISE

Leather
  Pocketbooks, bags—8½ to 10%
  Other manufactures of—4 to 14%
Mah jong sets—10%
Motorcycles—5%
Mushrooms, dried—3.2¢ lb. + 10%
Musical instruments
  Music boxes, wood—8%
  Woodwind, except bagpipes—7½%
  Bagpipes—Free
Paintings (works of art)
  Original—Free
  Copies, done entirely by hand—Free
Paper, manufactures of—8½%
Pearls
  Loose or temporarily strung and without clasp:
    Genuine—Free
    Cultured—2½%
    Imitation—20%
  Temporarily or permanently strung (with clasp attached or separate)—12 to 27½%
Perfume—8¢ lb. + 7½%
Postage stamps—Free
Printed matter—2 to 7%
Radios
  Transistors—10⅖%
  Other—6%
Rattan
  Furniture—16%
  Other manufactures of—12½%
Records, phonograph—5%
Rubber, natural, manufactures of—6%
Shaver, electric—6½%
Shell, manufactures of—8½%
Shoes, leather—2½ to 20%
Skis and ski equipment—8 to 9%
  Ski boots—Free to 20%

Customs Hints

Stereo equipment
 depending on components—5 to 12⅖%
Stones, cut but not set
 Diamonds not over one-half carat—4%
 Diamonds over one-half carat—5%
 Others—Free to 5%
Sweaters, of wool, over $5 per pound—37½¢ lb. + 20%
Tableware and flatware
 Knives, forks, flatware
  Silver—4¢ each + 8½%
  Stainless steel—1 to 2¢ each + 12½ to 45%
 Spoons, tableware
  Silver—12½%
  Stainless steel—17 to 40%
Tape recorders—5½ to 7½%
Toilet preparations
 Not containing alcohol—7½%
 Containing alcohol—8¢ lb. + 7½%
Toys—17½%
Truffles—Free
Vegetables, prepared—17½%
Watches, on $100 watch, duty varies from $6 to $13
Wearing apparel
 Embroidered or ornamented—21 to 42½%
 Not embroidered, not ornamented
  cotton, knit—21%
  cotton, not knit—8 to 21%
  linen, not knit—7½%
  manmade fiber, knit—25¢ lb. + 32½%
  manmade fiber, not knit—25¢ lb. + 27½%
  silk, knit—10%
  silk, not knit—16%
 wool, knit—37½¢ lb. + 15½ to 32%
 wool, not knit—25 to 37½¢ lb. + 21%
Wood
 Carvings—8%
 Manufactures of—8%

THE COMPLETE GUIDE TO A SUCCESSFUL CRUISE

Every effort has been made to indicate essential requirements; however, all regulations of customs and other agencies cannot be covered here in full.

Customs offices will be glad to advise you of any changes in regulations which may have occurred since publication of this book.

Should you need customs assistance while abroad, you can visit or telephone representatives located at the American Embassy or consulate in the following cities:

> London (499-900, extension 475)
> Paris (265-7400, extension 256)
> Rome (4674, extension 475)
> Frankfurt (0611 740071, extension 225)
> Bonn (02221 8955)
> Tokyo (583-7141, extension 590)
> Hong Kong (239-011, extension 243)
> Mexico City (525-9100, extension 687)
> Montreal (514 937-6301)

If you want to know about . . .

Passports. Contact the Passport Office, Department of State, Washington, D.C. 20524, or one of their regional offices located in Boston, Chicago, Los Angeles, Miami, New Orleans, New York, Philadelphia, San Francisco, and Seattle. Some clerks of court and postal clerks also issue passports.

Visas (if required). Get in touch with the appropriate embassy in Washington, D.C., or nearest consular office.

Inoculations. Contact your local or state health department.

Baggage allowance. Ask the cruise ship you are traveling on about this.

Customs Hints

Currency of other nations. Your local bank can be of assistance.

Foreign countries. For information about the country you will visit or about what articles may be taken into that country, contact the appropriate embassy, consular office or tourist information office.

District Directors of Customs are located in the following cities:

Anchorage, Alaska 99501
Baltimore, Md. 21202
Boston, Mass. 02109
Bridgeport, Conn. 06609
Buffalo, N. Y. 14202
Charleston, S.C. 24901
Chicago, Ill. 60607
Cleveland, Ohio 44199
Detroit, Mich. 48226
Duluth, Minn. 55802
El Paso, Texas 79985
Galveston, Texas 77550
Great Falls, Mont. 59401
Honolulu, Hawaii 96806
Houston, Texas 77052
Laredo, Texas 78040
Los Angeles, Calif. (see San Pedro)
Miami, Fla. 33132
Milwaukee, Wis. 53202
Minneapolis, Minn. 55401
Mobile, Ala. 36602
New Orleans, La. 70130
*New York, N. Y. 10048

---

*Write to Regional Commissioner of Customs.

Nogales, Ariz. 85621
Norfolk, Va. 23510
Ogdensburg, N. Y. 13669
Pembina, N. D. 58271
Philadelphia, Pa. 19106
Port Arthur, Texas 77640
Portland, Maine 04111
Portland, Oregon 97209
Providence, R. I. 02903
St. Albans, Vt. 05478
St. Louis, Mo. 63101
St. Thomas, V.I. 00801
San Diego, Calif. 92101
San Francisco, Calif. 94126
San Juan, P. R. 00903
San Pedro, Calif. 90732
Savannah, Ga. 31401
Seattle, Wash. 98104
Tampa, Fla. 33602
Washington, D. C. 20018
Wilmington, N. C. 24801

New customs breaks for the cruise traveler

The following is information for the traveling public about certain articles that may be brought into the United States, duty-free, from beneficiary developing countries under the U.S. Generalized System of Preferences (GSP).

GSP is a system used by many developed countries to help developing nations improve their financial or economic condition through export trade. It provides for the duty-free importation of a wide range of products from certain countries, which would otherwise be subject to customs duty. GSP went into effect in the United States on January 1, 1976, and will remain in effect until 1985.

GSP is administered by the Special Representative for Trade Negotiations in consultation with the secretary of state. The duty suspensions are proclaimed by the president under the Trade Act of 1974. The U.S. Customs Service is responsible for determining eligibility for duty-free entry under GSP.

Approximately 2,700 items have been designated as eligible for duty-free treatment from beneficiary developing countries (BCDs). The eligible articles are identified in the Tariff Schedules of the United States Annotated (1976) and the designated countries are also listed therein.

Under the Trade Act, many items, such as most footwear, most textile articles (including clothing), watches, some electronic products, and certain glass and steel products, are specifically excluded from GSP benefits.

For the traveler's convenience, an advisory list of the most popular tourist items which have been accorded GSP status is included in this section.

Ninety-eight nations and 40 dependent territories are currently designated as beneficiary developing countries. But articles produced by these countries may be excluded by Executive Order, if it is determined that their importation is harmful to domestic industry.

In addition, some articles from specified countries may be excluded from GSP treatment, if during the preceding year the level of imports of those articles exceeded $25 million, which may be adjusted according to changes in the U.S. gross national product for the preceding calender year ($29.9 million for 1976). Or they may be excluded if that country supplied 50 percent or more of the total U.S. imports of that product.

In order to take advantage of GSP, you must have

acquired the eligible article in the same beneficiary country where it was grown, manufactured, or produced. Articles may accompany you or may be shipped from the developing country *directly* to the United States.

On goods valued at more than $250, the District Director of Customs may require a Certificate of Origin (Form A), whether you ship the goods or bring them with you. If shipped, the goods should be accompanied by a commercial invoice in addition to Form A. This form would normally be obtained from the seller of the eligible article and must be signed by a properly designated official in the country of origin.

Such items as gin, liqueur, and perfume, if designated as eligible articles, may be subject to Internal Revenue tax despite their GSP status.

If merchandise claimed to be free of duty under GSP is found to be dutiable, you may include it in your customs exemption. Articles imported in excess of your exemption will be subject to duty. If you feel your article should have passed free of duty, you may write to the District Director of Customs where you entered, giving him the information concerning your entry. He will make a determination as to whether you are entitled to a refund.

Remember, as a returning U. S. resident, you may still bring in free of duty $100 worth of articles (fair retail value) acquired abroad in addition to those items covered by GSP. This exemption is $200 if you are returning from the U.S. Virgin Islands, American Samoa, or Guam. And keep in mind that all articles acquired abroad, whether free of duty or not, must be declared to U. S. Customs on your return.

Visitors or nonresidents are entitled to bring in articles which are duty-free under GSP, in addition to their basic customs exemption.

Customs Hints

If you have any questions about GSP, contact your nearest U.S. Customs office—there are almost 300 ports of entry throughout the United States. If you are overseas, the U.S. Embassy or consulate can be of assistance.

Popular tourist items

This listing is a guide to items designated as eligible for duty-free treatment under GSP which may be of interest to travelers for their personal use. Note that certain items from some beneficiary countries are excluded. When in doubt, check with your nearest customs office, or the American Embassy or consulate in the country you are visiting to verify the GSP status of an article you are considering bringing into the United States.

Bamboo, manufactures of (furniture not included)
Binoculars, prism; opera and field glasses
Cameras, motion-picture and still; lenses and other photographic equipment
Candy
Chinaware, bone; nonbone (tableware not included)
Cigarette lighters, pocket and table
Cork, manufactures of (except from Portugal)
Earthen tableware or stoneware, available in 77-piece sets and valued not over $12 per set (except in Romania)
Figurines, china
Flowers, artificial, of plastic or manmade fibers
Furs, wearing apparel, gloves, and other manufactures (other than manufactures excluded from Argentina)
Furniture, wood or plastic
Games, played on boards: chess, backgammon, darts, mah-jong
Golf balls and equipment

Ivory, beads and other manufactures of ivory (except from Hong Kong)

Jade, cut but not set for use in jewelry; other articles of jade

Jewelry of precious metal or stones; silver, chief value, valued not over $18 per dozen; other (except from Hong Kong)

Motorcycles

Music boxes

Musical instruments, except pianos

Paper, manufactures of

Pearls, cultured or imitation, loose or temporarily strung and without clasp

Perfume

Printed matter

Radio receivers, solid state (not for motor vehicles) (except from Republic of China, Hong Kong, Singapore, and Korea)

Rattan, manufactures other than furniture

Records, phonograph and tapes

Rubber, natural, manufactures of

Shaver, electric

Shell, manufactures of (except from the Philippines)

Silver, tableware and flatware

Skis and ski equipment (ski boots not included)

Stones (emeralds and diamonds not included), sapphires and rubies, cut but not set, suitable for use in jewelry (except from Thailand); semi-precious stones cut but not set, suitable for use in jewelry

Tape recorders

Toilet preparations (except bay rum and bay water from Bermuda)

Toys, not including dolls (except from Hong Kong)

Wood, carvings

Beneficiary countries

The countries listed below have been designated as

Customs Hints

beneficiary developing countries in the U.S. Generalized System of Preferences.

Independent Countries

Afghanistan	Guyana
Angola	Haiti
Argentina	Honduras
Bahamas	India
Bahrain	Israel
Bangladesh	Ivory Coast
Barbados	Jamaica
Benim	Jordan
Bhutan	Kenya
Bolivia	Korea, Republic of
Botswana	Lebanon
Brazil	Lesotho
Burma	Liberia
Burundi	Malagasy Republic
Cameroon	Malawi
Cape Verde	Malaysia
Central African Empire	Maldive Islands
	Mali
Chad	Malta
Chile	Mauritania
Colombia	Mauritius
Congo (Brazzaville)	Mexico
Costa Rica	Morocco
Cyprus	Mozambique
Dominican Republic	Nauru
Egypt	Nepal
El Salvador	Nicaragua
Equatorial Guinea	Niger
Ethiopia	Oman
Fiji	Pakistan
Gambia	Panama
Ghana	Papua New Guinea
Grenada	Paraguay
Guatemala	Peru
Guinea	Philippines
Guinea Bissau	Portugal

THE COMPLETE GUIDE TO A SUCCESSFUL CRUISE

Republic of China
 (Taiwan)
Romania
Rwanda
Sao Tome and
 Principe
Senegal
Sierra Leone
Singapore
Somalia
Sri Lanka
Sudan
Surinam
Swaziland
Syria

Tanzania
Thailand
Togo
Tonga
Trinidad and Tobago
Tunisia
Turkey
Upper Volta
Uruguay
Western Samoa
Yemen Arab Republic
Yugoslavia
Zaire
Zambia

Nonindependent Countries and Territories

Afars and Issas,
 French Territory of the
Antigua
Belize
Bermuda
British Indian Ocean
 Territory
British Solomon Islands
Brunei
Cayman Islands
Christmas Island
 (Australia)
Cocos (Keeling) Islands
Dominica
Falkland Islands
 (Malvinas) and
 Dependencies
French Polynesia
Gibraltar
Gilbert Island
Heard Island and
 McDonald Islands
Hong Kong

Macao
Montserrat
Netherlands Antilles
New Caledonia
New Hebrides Condominium
Niece
Norfolk Island
Pitcairn Island
Portuguese Timor
Saint Christopher-Nevis-
 Anguilla
Saint Helena
Saint Lucia
Saint Vincent
Seychelles
Spanish Sahara
Tokelau Islands
Trust Territory of the
 Pacific Islands
Turks and Chicos Islands
Tuvula
Virgin Islands, British
Wallis and Futuna Islands

Customs Hints

This section has been prepared as a guide for entry of noncommercial importations intended for personal use only. Details or requirements for commercial importers are not included.

22

Until We Meet Again

You will never be quite the same as you were before your cruise. New experiences will have left an indelible impression upon you. Your mind will be broadened by the experiences you've had and by the wonders you've seen. "Tension" and "anxiety" will have become words whose meaning escapes you. You will have made some new friends and become a better friend of yourself.

Now you will find yourselves, as you travel homeward, happily looking forward to greeting your old friends, to tackling your job with renewed vigor—and new insight—and to planning . . . another cruise, of course!

*Never a ship sails out of the bay
But carries my heart as a stowaway*
—Roselle Mercer Montgomery

Index

A

Abaft, 79
Above, 79
Aboveboard, 79
Achille Lauro, M.S., 121
Aft, 80
Agriculture, U.S. Dept. of, 143, 145
Air New Zealand, 106
Air/sea travel packages, 105–6
Alcoholic beverages, 22, 137, 139, 140, 142, 151
Alcohol, Tobacco and Firearms, U.S. Bureau of, 144
Alexander Pushkin, M.S., 122
Alfalfa tablets, 67–68
Alleyway, 80
Aloha shirt, 31
American Airlines, 106
American Bureau of Shipping, 97
Amidships, 80

Ammunition, 144
Anchor, 80
Andrews, Arthur, 13, 59
Angelina Lauro, M.S., *illus.* 121
Anniversaries, 5, 16–17, 77
Anticipation recipe, 13
Aquarius, M.S., *illus.* 118
Arcadia, 126
Art of Living excerpt, 69–70
Athwartship, 80
Attire. *See* Dress
Avast, 80

B

Backgammon, 25
Baggage, 6, 27, 29, 101–2, 103, 135–36, 146–47, 156
Baggage tags, 2, 135
Ballast, 80
Barber shop, 24
Barongs, 31

INDEX

Bathing suits, 29
Beam, 80
Beauty salon, 24, 30
Bell, 80
Bell buoy, 80
Below, 80
Bilge, 80
Bingo, 43
Birthdays, 5, 16–17, 77
Bitter end, 80
Bitts, 81
Boarding passes, 3, 5
Boarding time, 5–6
Boat drill, 81
Boheme, M.S., *illus.* 109
Bon voyage party, 3–5
Books, importation of, 143
Bow, 81
Box lunches, 20
Breakfast. *See* Meals
Breastline, 81
Bridge (game), 34
Bridge (ship), 81
Britanis, *illus.* 108
British Airways, 105
British Corporation Registry, 97
Buatier, Captain Piero, *illus.* 31
Buffet luncheon, 19
Bulkhead, 81
Bumboat, 81
Bunk, 81
Burke, Mike, 134

C

Cabin, 2–3, 8, 27, 81
Cable (radiogram), 2
Cable (rope), 81
Caffeine, 66, 67
Cambric tea, 20
Canberra, *illus.* 126
Capstan, 81
Captain, 81–82
Captain's Farewell Dinner, 24–25, 29, 30
Captain's table, 23–24

Captain's Welcome Aboard Cocktail Party, 22, 29, 30, *illus.* 31
Caribe, M.S., 109, *illus.* 36, 127
Carla "C," *illus.* 31, 62
Carnivale, *illus.* 42
Carras Cruises, *illus.* 107
Carried away, 82
Castalia, M.S., 118
Casual dress, 32
Caterers, ship's, 4
Champagne, 22
Champagne Night, 49
Chandris Lines Cruises, *illus.* 108
Chart, 82
Chart room, 82
Chasing the compass, 82
Chef, 25, 44
Chess, 35
Chow down, 82
Cigars and cigarettes, 137, 139, 140, 142
Classification societies, 97–98
Clothing. *See* Dress
Coaming, 82
Cocktails, 18, 22, 59
Coffee, morning, 18
Commend List, 23
Commodore Cruise Line Ltd.
 M.S. *Boheme*, *illus.* 109
 M.S. *Caribe*, 109, *illus.* 36
Companionway, 82
Compass, 82, 94–95
Constipation, 67–68
Continental Airlines, 106
Costa Lines
 Carla "C," *illus.* 31, 62
 Federico "C," *illus.* 110
 Italia, *illus.* 48
Costs, cruise, 106
Costume ball, 49–53
Costume parade, 50
Countess, *illus.* 112
Crew, 82
Crew show, 47, *illus.* 46
Cruise director, 6, 11, 33, 44, 50, 71–72

170

Index

Disembarkation Talk, 135
Cruise East
  M.S. *Rasa Sayang*, *illus.* 111
Cruise hostess, 6, 44
Cruise lines, 106, *illus.* 107–34.
  See also names of lines as
  Carras Cruises
Cruise staff, 6, 13, 82
Cunard Line
  Countess, *illus.* 112
  Princess, 112
  Queen Elizabeth, 112
Currency, xv, 146, 157
Customs, 135–65
  declaration, 104, 136–38
  duty rates, 150–56
  exemptions, 138–40
  offices, 156, 157–58
  restrictions, 141–46

D

Daily programs, 11, 13, 29, 33, 34, 59, 101
Danae, M.T.S., *illus.* 107
Dance classes, 43, 49
Dancing, 20, 25, 44
Daphne, M.T.S., *illus.* 107
Davits, 82
Davy Jones' locker, 82
Deadlight, 83
Dead reckoning, 83
Dead weight, 94
Deck, 83
Deck games, *illus.* 35
Deck plan, 2
Deck service, 19
Deck tennis, 35, *illus.* 36
Deep six, 83
Delta, M.S., *illus.* 47
Delta Airlines, 106
Delta Queen, *illus.* 113
Dental care, 64
Deviation errors, 94
Diets, special, 16–17
Dining. *See* Meals
Dinner at Sea, 30
Dinner in Port, 30, 31–32
Discotheque, 44

Disembark, 83, 101–2, 103–4, 135–36
Displacement, 93
Doctor, ship's 63, 65
Dog, 83
Donna Montserrat, M.S., *illus.* 12
Doric, S.S., *illus.* 4, 36, 45, 65, 72, 120
Draft, 83
Dramamine, 65–66
Dress, 24, 27–32, 102
  dress code, 29
  formal wear, 29–30, 32
Dressing ship, 83
Drugs, 146
Duty-free merchandise, 73, 137, 158–61
Duty rates, 150–56
Dysentery, 64

E

Eastern Steamship Lines
  Emerald Seas, *illus.* 40, 114
Elevenses, 19
Embarkation, 5–6, 83
Emerald Seas, *illus.* 40, 114
Entero Via Forma, 64
Entertainment, 11, 20, 25, 33–53
  Costume Ball, 49–53
  shows, 18, 44–49
Epirotiki Lines
  M.T.S. *Jason*, *illus.* 115
Etiquette, 61–62
Exercise classes, 42
Eyeglasses, 64

F

Fairsea, T.S.S., *illus.* 132
Fairway, 83
Fairwind, T.S.S., *illus.* 3, 132
Fantail, 83
Fathom, 83
Fathometer, 83
Fatigue, 66–67
Federico "C," M.S., *illus.* 110

INDEX

Fiorita, 108
Firearms, 144
Fisher, M.F.K., 61
Flagship Cruises
   M.S. *Kingshold*, *illus.* 116
Flagstaff, 83
Food. *See* Meals
Footwear, 27–28
Forecastle, 83
Foreign Assets Control, U.S. Office of, 145
Foreign Quarantine Program, 143
Formal dress, 29–30, 32
Forward, 84
Freshen the nip, 84
Fruit basket, cabin, 20–21

G

Galley, 84
Gambling, 43–44, 114, *illus.* 42
Games, 34–35, 49
Gangway, 84
Gastronomical Me, The, 61
Generalized System of Preferences (GSP), 142, 158–61
Germanischer Lloyd's, 97
German Rhine Line-Rhine Cruise, *illus.* 117
Gifts, duty-free, 141
God of the Feathered Serpent costume, 53
Godzilla, 84
Gold, importation of, 145
Golden Odyssey, M.S., *illus.* 38, 56, 130
Golf, *illus.* 37
Grand salon, 44
Guayaberas, 30
Gymnasium, *illus.* 65
Gyro-compass, 95

H

Handsomely, 84
Hardships, 75–76
Hatchway, 84
Hawse pipes, 84

Hawser, 84
Head, 84
Heave, 85
Heave to, 85
Hellenic Mediterranean Lines
   M.S. *Aquarius*, *illus.* 118
   M.S. *Castalia*, 118
Helm, 85
Hold, 85
Hold water, 85
Holidays, 5, 22, 23
Holland American Cruises. *See also* Monarch Cruise Lines
   M.S. *Prinsendam*, *illus.* 119
   S.S. *Rotterdam*, *illus.* 119
   S.S. *Statendam*, *illus.* 119
Holystone, 85
Home Lines
   S.S. *Doric*, *illus.* 4, 36, 45, 65, 72, 120
   S.S. *Oceanic*, *illus.* 19, 41, 120
Horse racing, 43, *illus.* 43
Hospital, ship's, 63
House flag, 85
Hunger, 18, 20–21

I

Immigration, 103–4
Inboard, 85
Infirmary, 63
Informal dress, 32
Inoculations, 64, 156
In-port meals, 30, 31–32
International Date Line, 98
Irish pennant, 85
Island Night, 49
Italia, *illus.* 48

J

Jason, M.T.S., *illus.* 115
Jogging, 35, *illus.* 67
Jolly Roger, 85
Jury rig, 85

K

Kazakhstan, M.S., *illus.* 122
Keel, 85
KLM Royal Dutch Airlines, 105
Knot, 85
Kungsholm, M.S., *illus.* 116

L

Ladder, 85
Landlubber, 86
Laundry, 29
Lazarette, 86
Lauro Line Cruises, *illus.* 121
Lectures, 42, 46, 58, 72, 135
Leeward, 86
Library, 35, *illus.* 41
Lifeboat, 86
Lifebuoy, 86
Light weight, 93
Line, 86
Liquor, 22, 137, 139, 140, 142, 151
Lloyd's Register of Shipping, 97
Log, 86
Lomotil, 64
Love Boat Cruises, 42
Lufthansa German Airlines, 105
Luggage, 27, 29, 101-2, 103, 135-36, 146-47, 156
Luggage tags, 2, 135
Lunch, 19, 20

M

Magnetic field, 94-95
Mail, 2
Maitre d', 5, 8, 16, 17, 20, 77, 78
March Shipping Corp. Cruises, *illus.* 12, 21
  M.S. *Alexander Pushkin*, 122
  M.S. *Kazakhstan*, *illus.* 122
  M.V. *Odessa*, 122
Mardi Gras, *illus.* 42

Meals, 8, 15-25, *illus.* 16, 21
  breakfast, 18
  dining room decor, 22-23, 24
  dress, 29, 30-32
  midnight buffet, 20
  room service, 18
  seating arrangements, 15-17
  sittings, 17-18
  snacks, 18, 19, 20-21
  special lunches, 19, 20
  tea time, 20
Medications, 63
Menus, 21-22
Midnight buffet, 20, 25
Mileage pool, 43
Mississippi Queen, *illus.* 113
Mizzenmast, 86
Monarch Cruise Lines, 119, *illus.* 60
Monarch Star, 119
Monarch Sun, 119, *illus.* 37
Money, xv, 146, 157
Monkey paw, 86-87
"Montezuma's Revenge," 64
Moor, 87
Movies, 17, 44

N

Narcotics, 146
National Airlines, 106
Nautical terms, 79-91
Negros Navigation Company Cruises, *illus.* 12, 123
Nordic Prince, *illus.* 129
Norwegian Caribbean Lines cruises, *illus.* 43
  M.S. *Sunward II*, *illus.* 124

O

Oceanic, S.S., illus. 19, 41, 120
Odessa, M.V., 122
Officers, ship's, 87
Old salt, 89
Open sitting, 18
Orchestra, 10, 11, 20, 44, 50-51
Oriana, 126
Orpheus, M.T.S., *illus.* 47

173

INDEX

Overhead, 87

P

Pacific Princess, illus. 126
Painter, 87
Panama Canal cruise, *illus.* 57
Pan American Airlines, 106
Paper, 6, 104
Paquet French Cruises
   M.S. *Renaissance, illus.* 125
Parlor games, 49
Passenger show, 48–49
Passports, 6, 156
Peninsular and Oriental Steam Navigation Co., 88, 126
   Arcadia, 126
   Canberra, illus. 126
   Oriana, 126
   Pacific Princess, illus. 126
Perfume, 140, 142, 154
Peterson, Wilfred A., 69–70
Philippine Airlines, 106
Photographer, ship's, 6–7, 10, 30
Photographic film, 147–48
Pier, 87
Pilot, 87
Pilot boat, 5
Ping-pong, 35
Pitch, 87
Plants, importation of, 144–45
Poolside service, 19, 20
Poop deck, 88
Port, 88
Porter, 4, 6
Porthole, 88
Ports of call, 55–58, 64
Posh, 88
Prescriptions, 63
Prince of Fundy Cruises, *illus.* 127
   M.S. *Caribe*, 109, *illus.* 36, 127
Princess, 112
Prinsendam, M.S., *illus.* 119
Printer, 11

Prudential Cruises, *illus.* 8, 128
   Santa Mariana, illus. 128
Purser's office, 5, 24, 78

Q

Quarter, 88
Queen Elizabeth, 112

R

Radiogram, 2
Raingear, 28
Rasa Sayang, M.S., *illus.* 111
Recipe for Anticipation, 13
Registro Nazionale Italiano, 97
Renaissance, M.S., *illus.* 125
Rivera, Eduardo, 53
Room service, 18
Rotterdam, S.S., *illus.* 119
Royal Caribbean Cruise Line ships, *illus.* 7, 38, 129
   Nordic Prince, illus. 129
   Song of Norway, illus. 129
   Sun Viking, illus. 129
Royal Cruise Lines, *illus.* 130
   M.S. *Golden Odyssey, illus.* 38, 56, 130
Royal topgallant sail, 88
Royal Viking Line, *illus.* 131
   Royal Viking Star, illus. 131
Rudder, 88
Rules of the road, 88
Running light, 89

S

Safety deposit boxes, 24
Salt, 89
Santa Mariana, illus. 128
Saunders, Jeraldine, vii, x–xi, *illus.* 12, 28, 31, 47, 62
Scenery, 53, *illus.* 52
Schooner, 89
Scrabble, 35
Screw, 89
Scupper, 89
Scuttlebut, 89

Index

Sea dog, 89
Seams, 89
Seasickness, 65
"Seas of Ulysses" Mediterranean cruise, *illus.* 56
Serpentine, 10
Sextant, 89
Shaft, 89
Shipping of merchandise, 148–50
Shipshape, 89
Shoes, 27–28
Shopping, x, 32, 71–73, 146. *See also* Customs
  shipping merchandise, 148–50
  ship's shop, 32, 72–73, *illus.* 72
Shore excursions, 55–58, 64
Shot (inoculation), 64, 156
Shot (measurement), 89
Show a leg, 89
Shuffle board, *illus.* 34
Sick bay, 90
Singles party, 59–60
Sitmar cruise ships, *illus.* 9, 16, 40, 41, 132
  T.S.S. *Fairsea, illus.* 132
  T.S.S. *Fairwind, illus.* 3, 132
Skeet shooting, *illus.* 36
Skin, 90
Skipper, 90
Sky pilot, 90
Snacks. *See* Meals
Social activities, 11, 30, 33–53
Sommelier, 22
Song of Norway, illus. 129
Sounding, 90
Splice the main brace, 90
Sports director, 6
Starboard, 90
Statendam, S.S., *illus.* 119
Stateroom, 2–3, 8, 27, 81
Steamboat cruises, *illus.* 113
Stella Maris, 133
Stella Oceanis, illus. 133
Stella Solaris, illus. 133

Stem, 90
Stern, 90
Steward, 4, 7, 16, 18, 20, 23, 77, 78
Sugar, 64–65, 67
Sun Line cruise ships, *illus.* 46, 67, 133
  Stella Maris, 133
  Stella Oceanis, illus. 133
  Stella Solaris, illus. 133
Sun over the yardarm, 90
Suntan lotion, 66
Sun Viking, illus. 129
Sunward II, M.S., *illus.* 124
Superstructure, 90
Swan (W.F. and R.K.) Ltd. cruise ships, *illus.* 47
Swimming pool, 35, *illus.* 38, 40
Swimwear, 29

T

Tablemates, 17, 25
Taffrail, 90
Tar, 90
Tea time, 20
Telephone service, 2
Ten Commandments, Passengers', xv–xvi
Tenders, 57–58, 90
Theme cruises, 42
Thwart, 90
Thwartship, 80
Tiller, 90
Tipping 6, 17, 18, 77–78
Tonnage, 93–94
"Touristas," 64
Tours, port, 56–58
Trans World Airlines, 106
Trapshooting, 35
Travel agent, 55–56, 64, 105–6
Trick, 91
Turn to, 91
Twice laid, 91

U

Underway, 91

INDEX

United Airlines, 106
Unship, 91
Up behind, 91

V

Variation, 94
Visas, 156
Visitors, 3, 4, 5, 10
Vitamin B, 65, 66
Vitamin C, 63, 66
Vitamin tablets, 66

W

Waiter, 17, 77–78
Waiting lists, 55–56
Wake, 91
Walco, Mort, 5
Walkathons, 35

Wardrobe. *See* Dress
Warp, 91
Watch, 91
Water, 64
Water breaker, 91
Weigh anchor, 91
Weight, 93–94
Well Wishers, International, 5
Western Airlines, 106
Whistle, 91
Windjammer "Barefoot" Cruises, *illus.* 134
Windward, 91
Wines, 22
Wine steward, 22, 78

Y

Yaw, 91
Yogurt, 64

Made in the USA
San Bernardino, CA
21 December 2014